Financial Abundance

Real-Life Stories
That Inspire
Your Path to Prosperity

CONNIE COSTANZO

Financial Abundance: Real Life Stories That Inspire Your Path to Prosperity
Published by Connie Costanzo
Cleveland, Ohio

ISBN: 979-8-9915103-0-1
BUSINESS & ECONOMICS / Finance / Wealth Management

Cover and Interior design by Victoria Wolf, wolfdesignandmarketing.com. Edited by Gail Kerzner, The Savvy Red Pen, thesavvyredpen.com. Copyright owned by Connie Costanzo.

Give yourself little things to look forward to.

Always! Every day!

It brings hope. It brings joy!

This book is dedicated to my mom and dad, whose love and consistent encouragement throughout my life have touched my heart in unforgettable ways. Because of you, I am who I am and aspire to be even more. Thank you for being the best parents in the world!

I love you!

CONTENTS

FOREWORD

YOU'VE JUST PICKED UP AN AMAZING BOOK that's about to transform your financial journey. Congratulations on making this fantastic choice to dive into *Financial Abundance*.

When it comes to making financial decisions, things can get pretty overwhelming. Connie's book is your roadmap to creating confidence and financial freedom. Her approach is refreshingly honest and deeply understanding of the unique challenges and aspirations we all face, especially women.

From the moment you start reading, you'll see why Connie Costanzo is such a remarkable advisor. She's not what you might think of as a typical financial advisor. She brings heart, passion, and an unshakeable commitment to everything she does. (Seriously, she's the kind of person who commits and follows through on every promise.)

Financial Abundance isn't just another finance book filled with jargon and dry advice. Connie fills these pages with sincerity, real-life stories, and practical tips that make sense. She breaks down complex topics like financial planning, investments, life insurance, and annuities into simple fundamentals that you can understand and provides actionable steps.

One of the most powerful aspects about this book is Connie's belief in the transformative power of education. She equips you with the knowledge you need to make informed decisions and take control of your financial future. And she does it all with a warmth and clarity that makes you feel like you're having a chat with a trusted friend.

I've had the pleasure of working with Connie, and let me tell you, she's the real deal. Her insights and guidance have been invaluable, and I'm thrilled to see her sharing her wisdom through this book.

As you read *Financial Abundance*, you'll find yourself inspired and empowered to take charge of your finances. Connie's stories of success and interviews with professionals from various fields provide a treasure trove of tips and lessons that you can apply immediately.

This book isn't just about numbers. It's about creating a life of abundance, security, and fulfillment. Connie's approach to financial planning is transformational. She shows us that with the right knowledge and mindset, we can achieve financial empowerment and live the life we've always dreamed of.

So, get comfortable, grab a cup of coffee, and get ready to embark on a journey that will change the way you think about money. Connie is here to guide you every step of the way, and you couldn't be in better hands.

Happy reading!

Robyn Crane, CFP®
Keynote Speaker
4X #1 Best Selling Author
Business Coach for Financial Professionals

INTRODUCTION

Begin with the end in mind.

— STEVEN COVEY

IMAGINE WAKING UP ONE MORNING to the news that you've inherited $100 million! Money is no longer a concern! You're financially free!

What dreams would you pursue? What passions would you chase? Where would your newfound freedom take you?

I think it's important to ask ourselves questions like this. It gets us to dream a little and shoot for the stars, right?

What would you look forward to? What would you do for yourself? What would you do for others?

Would you **travel the world and** explore exotic destinations, immerse yourself in different cultures, and visit iconic landmarks? What about considering luxury cruises, private tours, and extended stays in places you've always dreamed of visiting?

Would you explore fine dining and gourmet restaurants or hire a personal chef to prepare your meals at home? You could even take a culinary tour around the world.

Or how about pampering yourself with luxury spa treatments or high-end shopping? Or treating yourself to thrilling activities such as skydiving, surfing, or skiing?

Would you take up painting, sculpting, writing, pursuing your artistic self?

Maybe you'd invest in real estate. Buy properties in beautiful locations around the world that you can enjoy or rent out when you're not using them.

Or support causes that are near and dear to your heart: Invest time and resources in philanthropic activities. Establish a foundation, support charities, or volunteer for causes you're passionate about.

Or maybe you'd create a legacy by investing in an extraordinary project that leaves a lasting impact, like writing a book, launching a business, or supporting groundbreaking startups.

Maybe you think these visions are extravagant—and perhaps some of them are— but my point is that with financial concerns out of the way, you can focus on enriching your life experiences and making a positive impact on the world around you.

This book aims to demystify the complexities of financial planning, offering clear advice to help you grow your wealth and achieve the financial security you've always dreamed of.

This book is also designed to get you to recognize and get rid of any of your own negative thoughts surrounding money. It's an invitation to empower you and get you to start thinking differently— more open-mindedly—about financial independence and wealth.

HOW THIS BOOK WAS BORN

When a mentor, Robyn Crane, first suggested I write a book, my immediate reaction was, "There's *no* way I, Connie Costanzo, can write a book. First of all, who am *I* to be writing a book, especially when there are lots of financial planning books in the market? What would be unique about mine? Second, although I have a clear vision of what I want to communicate, I am acutely aware I am not an experienced author. (Thank God for my editor)! These notions gave me pause.

However, I felt a strong prompting to reconsider and move forward. My true passion lies in educating my clients and demonstrating the power of aligning their finances with their goals. I realized that people need my distinctive approach and my unique personality, qualities that set this book apart. They need someone who can not only simplify complex financial concepts but also make them relatable and engaging. Someone who is genuine and compassionate but also fun to work with. Someone who digs a little deeper into what the goals are. Witnessing the positive transformation in my clients' lives because of my advice reaffirms my love for what I do. I asked myself, "How can I maximize that impact?" Writing a book was the answer. Through this medium, I can reach a wider audience by providing the essential knowledge that people often lack because sometimes we just don't know what we don't know. Knowledge is key.

I SET OUT ON A MISSION

I knew I wanted engaging interviews to be a major, unique component of the book because I believe we resonate with true stories from those who may be just like us. Stories touch our hearts and change us. And sharing them can impact us significantly.

Since I primarily work with executives, particularly women, I decided to leverage LinkedIn to reach out to them. I contacted complete strangers with executive or professional titles to gather their insights on money—their challenges and successes. I also reached out to women I know and respect, asking if they would be willing to be interviewed for a book about money. I encouraged them to candidly share their thoughts. To ensure their comfort and confidence in their transparency, I offered the option to use an alias. Some chose to remain anonymous, while others were comfortable sharing their identity. Their answers to my questions are refreshingly honest and transparent, and I thank them for that.

You'll also see the interviewees'"Words of Wisdom" along with my comments, "Connie's Insights."

The women (and the few men) I had the privilege to interview were more than willing to share their experiences, hoping you might find a golden nugget in their story and be able to identify something that worked for them to implement into your own life. *My* hope is that their stories resonate with you and that you might see yourself in their experiences. I believe in the power of relatable stories. They can spark those "aha" moments that make us think, "Yes, that's just like me." or "Wow! That's a great idea. I should try that."

GUIDING YOU THROUGH THE JOURNEY OF THIS BOOK

Traditional Chapters

In Chapter 1, I share the transformative power of financial planning by introducing you to four stories of real people who overcame their financial challenges by implementing effective strategies. As you read these scenarios, see if you can identify with any of the experiences.

Chapter 2 is all about me and money. You'll get to know a little about my family background, my money mindset, my entrepreneurial journey, and my passion for working with my clients, especially women. Get ready for some shocking statistics and some annoying myths about women and money.

Think of Chapters 3-6 as your primer on the basics of financial planning: We talk about financial planning, investing, life insurance, and annuities. I also offer ideas on how you might implement various options to improve your own financial situation. At the end of each chapter, I share a story on how implementing the concept has improved that person's life.

THE INTERVIEWS

Between chapters 1-6, you'll find the treasure trove of the engaging interviews I mentioned previously—Personal Money Stories, Parts 1-6. They are grouped together according to the most appropriate theme discussed in the chapters surrounding them. Keep in mind the interviews were done over a one-year period when the stock market had some challenges during the COVID-19 crisis.

THE BONUSES IN THE BACK

Crunching the Numbers: Calculating Your Retirement Needs is a valuable worksheet you can use to figure out how much you need for retirement. What makes it fun is that you can put your own financial numbers in the blanks and figure out your basic needs, and then you will know what you "need" to plan for. Then you can put your "dream" numbers into the formula and figure out what it might take to realize some of your dreams. You may be surprised at how attainable your numbers can be with a little planning. Why is it a great exercise? Because it is your reality. Your dream retirement is likely within your reach, and you might be able to prove that to yourself.

The Power of Compounding worksheet is memorable. If I gave you the choice, would you like a million dollars today or one penny doubled every day? The chart showing the growth on paper is astounding! And that's the power of compounding!

ACTION PLAN

My **Action Plan** lays out next steps if you choose to reach out and want to continue the conversation with me. Even if it's not with me, let it be with someone who's an expert and can guide you to your own financial wealth.

You'd go to a doctor for your physical and mental health, right? And to a contractor to remodel your home? They're experts in their fields. A financial advisor is the expert who can help you with the financial aspect of your life.

WE SHOULD ALL DARE TO DREAM. And once we achieve financial stability and security, I believe that God places even greater dreams in our hearts. With our financial foundations secure, we can be open to even greater possibilities that enable us to contribute more meaningfully to our society and to the world.

So, let's dare to dream bigger and take it to the next level.

Do you accept the dare? If so, I'm with you every step of the way. Let's begin!

CHAPTER 1

Your Future Starts Here

The Best Way to Predict the Future is to Create it.

—ABRAHAM LINCOLN

YOU HAVE MONEY! You want freedom, independence, and security for your future. You want financial stability! And you want the certainty of knowing you're making the best decisions about your money! You probably want to have a little fun, too, and dream a little on the way!

Small changes can make a big difference! Creating a plan is the key. But why don't more people do it? The answer isn't the same for everyone, but there are some common reasons.

Often, we have pre-conceived notions or fears regarding money, which could be preventing us from deciding how to move forward.

We are afraid of taking steps in any direction because we don't want to make a mistake. Some of us are embarrassed, believing we ought to be further along in the process than we are. Some of us may have everything we want and resist new thoughts or ideas, thinking we're better off handling it on our own. In other cases, we may not have enough information to feel confident. If any of this resonates with you, know that you are not alone.

LET ME TELL YOU A STORY.

A 66-year-old woman approached me with great enthusiasm, having accumulated approximately $900,000 for her retirement. The time had come. She was planning to retire the following year. With that money and some other assets and funds, she was a millionaire! What an accomplishment!

She worked all her life to save for her retirement. And there she was. That precious moment she had been waiting for had arrived, the day she could finally stop working and start really enjoying life. Not that she hadn't been enjoying her life all along. She had, but now … the next important chapter would begin. She was looking forward to it and couldn't wait for the many amazing adventures to come!

Her Concerns:

She wanted ideas about what she should do with the money she had saved for so long to ensure her standard of living moving forward. She needed to be confident she wouldn't run out of money.

The Process:

We talked about her priorities, exploring her dreams and goals. We also discussed how she envisioned enjoying life—what she wanted to do and fund for in retirement. What an enjoyable conversation!

What We Implemented and the Results:

We put a portion of her monies into **her own savings** so it would always be there for her. That would give her peace of mind. If she ever needs anything, she can get to this money right away.

Then we took another portion of her retirement monies and **set up a strategy that could guarantee* her additional income each year along with her social security income.** Guaranteed income is important to her, and it makes sense because she's more at ease knowing exactly what she can spend each year.

We took the largest portion of her money and rolled it over into **a new retirement account tied to the stock market.** By doing this, we keep most of her money growing so it keeps up with inflation, which is essential. Sure, she's aware the market will have its ups and downs, but she's comfortable doing this and is now confident in her ability to retire.

Now the fun begins! She feels more secure knowing she has a plan, and over the years, she'll be able to enjoy her retirement the way she dreamed it would be.

We created three avenues for her money:
+ **One that is liquid,**
+ **One that ensures guaranteed* income,**
+ **And one that will continue growing in the stock market.**

I look forward to being there for her every step of the way as we continue to work together and maintain her confidence and comfort.

HERE'S ANOTHER SUCCESS STORY I'M HAPPY TO BE A PART OF.

A professional 42-year-old woman is making a nice living and happy with her present life. She works hard, and her field allows her to travel the world. She's doing a stellar job of putting money away using her company 401k and into a savings account she had set up on her own.

Her Concerns:

In addition to the 401k savings with her employer, she had about $100,000 in a savings account. She knew that was probably not the best place for the money but wasn't sure what else to do. She was so busy she had no time to even think about it. Another one of her goals was to "see into the future"—to have a plan in place, to know if she was short in funding the kind of retirement she was dreaming of. This way, she could make small changes now, if necessary, that would guarantee her security and independence for her financial future.

The Process:

When we sat down to chat about what was most important to her, she shared with me, with a twinkle in her eye, that her dream when she retires is to travel. She truly enjoys her life as it is, but travel is primarily for work right now. She would love to be able to travel for leisure when she is retired.

We talked about other important things, like not having to rely on anyone to care for her when she grows old. She wanted to know if she should think about and prepare for assisted living, not that she would want or even need it, but it's wise to hope for the best and prepare for the worst. In the worst-case scenario, she wants to be able to take care of herself and be financially independent. She does *not* want to have to worry about money—ever! So, together we planned.

What We Implemented and the Results:

As we continued our conversations, she decided, based on my recommendations, to leave a good chunk of money (an amount she was comfortable with) in her **savings account** to allow it to continue earning a small amount of interest. This money is available to her if she needs it in a hurry.

We then put a large chunk of her money into an investment **account she's comfortable being a bit more aggressive with**. She can still get to it if an opportunity arises or if she absolutely needs it. It remains in a liquid account that can grow.

Because she wants to travel **later when she retires, we set up a wealth-building strategy using a permanent life insurance policy** that she contributes to each month. While it offers an essential death benefit, it also acts as a guaranteed* savings account that she can pull from—tax-free— when she's ready. Now she will be able to vacation each year in the future to wherever she wants. Not only that, but if she needs the funds for something else, she still has access to it. It's her money, and it grows within the account that provides liquidity, safety, predictable rates of return, and tax advantages.

We set up several strategies that align with her goals. Having a solid plan in place gave her confidence and freedom in her financial future. The strategies we implemented can also help cover the need for assisted living or that type of care should she need it down the road. We can always add appropriate vehicles as life continues to change.

3 strategies used to get her started toward her goals:

- **Ensure she maintains a comfortable amount of liquid funds in her savings for emergencies.**
- **Invest more aggressively to keep pace with inflation and achieve growth.**
- **Develop a wealth building strategy using life insurance.**

This relationship—and all my client relationships—mean the world to me. It's fulfilling to be their partner, looking toward their future with excitement! Watching and helping them see the possibility of so much they can look forward to, as well as protecting what they already have, brings me so much joy. It's why I do what I do! And it's why I encourage you, too, to find a savvy financial advisor who can help you create the life of your dreams.

HERE IS ANOTHER POWERFUL STORY.

A lovely couple came to me with $1,000,000 that was nicely nestled into a savings account. They loved just knowing it was there. They recognized it might not be the wisest place to have this much money in a savings account, but they weren't sure of the options and best strategies to optimize it.

They had been looking for a financial advisor but couldn't find one they felt comfortable with—until we met. This couple was ready to make some changes! He wanted to retire in about ten years. She had no intention of retiring … just yet. They knew they wanted to do something significant with their money and create their retirement plan.

Their Concerns:

The challenge of a million dollars in a savings account is that they could be missing out by not utilizing the variety of savings and investment vehicles available to them. In addition, because they make a lot of money, they pay a lot in income taxes, so we needed to solve for that as well.

The Process:

We sat down and had a meaningful conversation. We started by talking about what was important to them—their frustrations, challenges, concerns, and short- and long-term goals. They wanted to know what options would best serve them, especially those that would best optimize the wealth they had built so far.

What We Implemented and the Results:

Based on my recommendations, they decided to keep roughly one quarter of their savings in the **savings account** for security and liquidity. That was important to them. They felt secure knowing the money is there if needed.

Important Tip:

Banks that provide FDIC insurance (Federal Deposit Insurance Corporation) will insure up to $250,000 per depositor, per account ownership type. This means if you have $1,000,000 at the bank in one account, you are guaranteed $250,000 if that bank falters. So, in my opinion, it's better to have multiple accounts up to $250,000 in the same bank or to split your money at different banks.

Then they decided to put a specific amount of that savings **into an investment vehicle** that would still be liquid but more geared for growth. They wanted a little more of an aggressive investment strategy for that part of their money.

The next chunk of the money went into **an ultra-conservative account** but could still earn more than keeping it in the bank. If they want to use the money for emergencies or opportunities that come along, they are ready.

As you can see, this is an effective strategy for them because they effectively divided their savings into "pieces" and had a different goal for each portion.

These strategies work well for them, but they had one more major concern. As I noted, they were paying a lot in income taxes each year because they both make a significant amount of money. She owns her own business, so this allowed us to open **a retirement account** that works much like a 401k, and she started contributing to it. This is a **tax-advantaged vehicle** for her, and it's exactly what they needed. By doing that, they save a bundle in taxes, and that makes them very happy!

Something else they had not thought about: She didn't have any life insurance, so there is no protection for the plan we just laid in place. If something were to happen to her, he would no longer have her income to count on. So, in addition to the emotional devastation, it would create an immediate financial strain on him.

Taking care of the matters involved with the death of a loved one is an immediate financial burden. That would be just the start. Without life insurance protection in place, her death would surely impact him short- and long-term. Ultimately, their goals, his current lifestyle, and any plans they made to leave a legacy would be affected.

So, we set up something I like to call **a wealth-building permanent life insurance policy** for her. This provides a death benefit and does something else quite special. Part of the premium is used for the death benefit, and part goes to a "cash" account that can increase and grow over time. It effectively creates a tax-free bucket for them to pull cash from or income from whenever they want to down the road. For their goals, the plan is to use this special life insurance policy as a retirement supplement to income. They pay no tax on what they take when we set it up this way. This is a significant bucket for them because much of what they have planned for as retirement income will be taxed when they take it. Having another source of income they can take from tax-free is so powerful!

Strategies we used:

- **Retain one-quarter of their savings as liquid emergency funds.**
- **Establish an investment account focused on growth to keep pace with inflation.**

- Create a conservative, liquid investment account.
- Set up a SIMPLE plan for her, similar to a 401k with tax advantages.
- Develop a wealth-building account using life insurance to provide tax-free income during retirement.

In summary, this plan helps this couple in so many ways—not only to achieve some short-term goals but also to get them set for their long-term retirement goals! Identifying a key piece that protects all that they have planned for was missing and helping them fix it was a significant benefit to them.

When you have a solid savings amount to work with, there is so much a financial advisor can do to help set you up for financial success and freedom for your future. By utilizing different strategies that make sense, they can help prepare you to have a wonderful retirement and create confidence and security along the way while looking towards the future together as a team!

HERE'S ONE MORE STORY BEFORE WE MOVE ON.

I met with a delightful couple, ages 65 and 66. He loved his work, but she, not so much. She was almost ready to retire but was concerned whether they would have enough available guaranteed income when it was time.

The Problem:

They hadn't worked with a financial planner before but were eager for ideas and wanted to be sure they would be financially secure for the rest of their lives. They wanted a future with the flexibility to travel, dine out, and enjoy other fun activities together at their leisure.

The Process:

After reading the stories above, I'm sure you already know where we were going to begin. Yes, you are correct! We started first with a conversation about what was important to them. That's pivotal.

When I met with this couple, we talked about different ways they could have a guaranteed* income in addition to the social security income they would be receiving. And I shared different strategies and options they could put in place to ensure financial freedom and security for their future. They were thrilled!

What We Implemented and the Results:

The strategy of **using an annuity** was part of their answer. Together, they had about $750,000 in retirement funds and pensions. What we did for them, and especially for her, was to put her mind at ease by putting a good portion of that money into an annuity—not just any annuity, but an **Equity Indexed Annuity**. An annuity can guarantee* income annually. And the Equity Indexed Annuity guarantees no loss of principal from year to year.

With their social security income and the income they know they can take from the annuity, they can have a guaranteed* amount when they retire, and that makes them so happy.

So, what will they do with the rest of the retirement money and pensions they have accumulated over the years?

For her, we transferred her old pension and retirement account into **a new retirement account.** Once he retires, we will move the money currently in his part of his company's retirement account into a new retirement account for him. This way, the money continues to grow because it's active in the stock market, and this portion of their wealth in the stock market will likely keep up with inflation. Keeping up with inflation is a significant strategy in any balanced portfolio.

Why would we transfer to a new account with us? The answer is simple. We want it to grow. And we want to keep an eye on it for and with them. If no one is looking after their money for them, which usually happens when you leave employment, it only makes sense for them to transfer those monies to us so we can help the money grow. It's part of my fiduciary responsibility.

One key benefit of working with a boutique RIA firm (Registered Investment Advisor) like mine that many people don't know is the freedom to invest in a wide range of options. With a 401(k) or standard retirement account there are often limits on the investment options available to you, but working with an RIA firm allows much more flexibility.

They now sleep more soundly at night because they are confident their financial future is secure. They have done the work to get the right strategies in place so they know exactly what they can expect in the future, and that is freeing to them.

Strategies that work for them:

- Open an annuity that will provide guaranteed income when she needs it.
- Create a new rollover account for her that is expected to grow and keep pace with inflation.
- Eventually establish a new rollover account for him that is also expected to grow.

Getting your affairs in order is life-changing! You give yourself a wonderful future by doing it!

I SHARE THESE FOUR STORIES WITH YOU to give you some insight into what financial planning has been able to do for others and what it can do for you. If you're open to ideas and strategies when it comes to your money, this book is definitely for you. All it takes is a little planning—and a savvy advisor.

Throughout the book, I share valuable information you can start to use today! You can take control of your financial future and create the emotional and financial security you desire. I also share some economic principles that will help you make sound decisions about your money.

How amazing would it be to have the knowledge to make some of your biggest dreams come true? With a little discipline and courage, overcoming any negative thoughts you may have been taught about money, you can begin living the life you dream of.

We all have money challenges—whether you're among the wealthiest of the wealthy or struggling to make ends meet. We all must make decisions about money every day. Will they be *good* decisions or *great* decisions? Will your choices safeguard your money or grow it? Maybe both. There's no right or wrong answer. It depends on you and your situation.

Will the decisions you make add joy to your life? And could they also bring joy to others? The better you are with your money, the more it can grow, and the more you can impact your own life and the lives of others around you.

Let's explore your current situation.

+ What do you want that you don't already have?
+ What challenges, fears, and frustrations are you facing?
+ When unforeseen things happen or when exciting opportunities come along, do you have the cash to take advantage of them?
+ Do you have money all over the place—in real estate, the stock market, your checking, and your savings? Is it being optimized?
+ Perhaps you started a Roth account a long time ago but haven't added much to it. Is that bad?
+ Remember that old 401k account from long ago that's just sitting there? Who's helping you look after that?
+ Is anything holding you back from having the life that you want?

Let's ask some more questions:

+ When you get to retirement, is there a way to know you won't run out of money?
+ How much money do you need so that you know you will absolutely—positively—be secure in the future?

- What investments should you consider? Are you investing in the right things?
- Are there certain things you should be doing now that you don't know about?
- Is there anything you could be doing better?

Let's also ask an all-empowering question:

- What can I do to ensure myself the emotional freedom that comes with being financially free?

It all starts with a plan—a solid financial plan. Ben Franklin said, "People don't plan to fail. They just fail to plan."

So, let's get started. It's as easy as ...

Step 1: Create a vision for your future.

Step 2: Get a strategy in place to accomplish it.

Step 3: Execute it. Step by step. Implement one strategy at a time.

IN THE PAGES AHEAD, you'll get an intimate, candid look into real people's experiences, exploring their frustrations, challenges, and concerns about money. You'll also hear about their hopes and dreams and get a look at their different mindsets around money. Some prefer safety over risk and vice versa. Others like to diversify by investing in the stock market and real estate. Some are wealthy; some are not. And some are in between. Many have shared their mistakes, and as they look back, they share how they might have made different decisions.

I hope these stories will resonate, inspire, and truly empower you. Who do you identify with? What lessons can you learn from them? When we share our experiences, we can significantly impact each other. I appreciate my interviewees' transparency and willingness to share. Each of them contributed to this book in unique ways.

Let's dig in.

PERSONAL MONEY STORIES PART 1

MARTA

Age: 38

Current Position: Chartered Global Management Accountant, FCMA, CGMA, BA (Hons) ODCP

Q: What's most important to you about money?

A: For a long period of time, I was careless with my money. And here is why; In 2014 I lost my partner, and it changed my mindset overnight with my personal money outlook. I am a financial professional and I am very forward thinking. However, personally, my partner was always the one thinking of saving for the pension and putting money away. When he died, I thought, what is the point of saving for my pension? I don't care anymore, and I am going to spend my money and travel and try to find joy. What is the use of saving if you never know what life is going to bring. You must enjoy life while you have it. I tried to travel every single weekend. To experience people and life was how I coped with the loss. At the same time my company was paying my pension, so I knew I had money being put away for my future. When this happened though it was a shock and very difficult for me.

Q: What do you really want that you don't have right now?

A: I'd really like to buy a house. I have money for a deposit, but in my head, I struggle with long term commitment. A 20-year mortgage is hard to commit to. I don't like debt! I need to know that I will be able to pay it off quickly. The fact that I have savings gives me flexibility.

Q: What's your next big goal? What's the next level for you?
A: From an investment point of view, I need to sort out where I am going with my pension and everything I have. I will be 40 soon and I am thinking of traveling around the world, and to celebrate myself, that I am alive and in my 40s. I want to be happy according to my definition of happiness. In every day, I want to find something that could be like, wow, that was amazing. The joy!

Q: If you could wave a magic wand, what does life look like for you?
A: I think I would love to have a house with a beautiful view. Right now, I have a beautiful view even though I am renting. I have seven weeks of holiday. I don't see myself with children but a house full of friends and a lot of love.

Q: Have you ever worked with a financial advisor/planner before?
A: No. I am good at financial planning with business, but I haven't worked with anyone because I haven't been ready yet. It has changed now, and I would like to work with a financial advisor.

Q: What do you think you would like best about working with them?
A: I would like to have options and scenarios for what I can do to influence the future.

LET'S TALK ABOUT SOME CHALLENGES, FEARS, AND FRUSTRATIONS.

Q: What's your number one concern?

A: Health is my number one concern—my health and the health of people around me. It's not money because I am privileged to have enough money, but I want to be happy and healthy. I am healthy and want to continue being healthy.

Q: What do you know now that you wish you would have known early on?

A: I should have started to put money away to invest earlier. At least ten years ago, if I'd put money away while still enjoying life, I would be that much better off now.

Marta's Words of Wisdom: Don't compare yourself to others because every person is on an individual unique journey. One person is happy to save 50% for the future, but another will want to go on a holiday. You can't say one is right and one is wrong. We are each on our own unique path.

Connie's Insights: Marta was lovely to interview. Her story brought tears to my eyes. Losing her partner was a devastating event that brought her heartbreak. However, that event caused Marta to have a change in her thinking. She decided to begin balancing both saving and enjoying the life she was living.

WENDY DAVIS

Age: 62

Current Position: President, Corporate Gifting
Company for Fortune 500 companies

Q: What's most important to you about money?
A: I would say managing for the household. I had hang-ups with money and the lack of it when I was growing up. We never had enough. I lived with a blue- collar family and didn't want to ask for money from my parents, ever. I was taught that people who make money cheat other people.

Q: What do you really want that you don't have right now?
A: A scalable business.

Q: What's your next big goal, What's the next level for you?
A: Security, that there is enough, that we won't run out of money. I have assets of $2 million right now, and I want to double that to $4 million in one year. In ten years from now, 10 million is the financial goal.

Q: If you could wave a magic wand, what would life look like right now?
A: I would be working part time spending time with my hubby enjoying life. I would have people in the right places within the business to facilitate so that I could work part-time.

Q: Have you ever had a financial planner?
A: Yes, I do. I really enjoy the relationship we have built through the years.

Q: How has it helped you get to where you are today?
A: It's everything! I have a high trust when he makes recommendations. I love that I can trust him and the security it brings to me.

Q: What else would you like from your financial advisor that would make your experience even more valuable?
A: He always asks what's coming up for us, so that he can better recommend. I might like to have more recommendations from him. And for him to break it down into baby steps for me. He doesn't throw many things at us at once and I like that. He gives us thoughtful consideration on succession planning, and things like philanthropy. I love that my accountant and financial advisor get together in the same room. And I like to be able to have them both there with me. Working toward the common goal.

LET'S TALK ABOUT SOME CHALLENGES, FEARS, AND FRUSTRATIONS.

Q: What's the biggest thing holding you back or slowing you down from reaching your big goals?

A: I'd say it's my thoughts and beliefs around money. I get in my own head sometimes with negative thoughts. I must constantly remind myself that it's okay to make a lot of money.

Q: What one challenge do you have that you would love to be solved right now?

A: I wish the stock market would get better and to have marketing in place to scale my business.

Q: What do you know now that you wish you would have known early on?

A: That it's okay to invest in my business. I would have loved to have a woman as a business role model. I was taught the scarcity mindset, not to spend money but to save everything. I go against that today. But it's deliberate for me. It's okay to spend, and you must. How else will you grow?

Wendy's Words of Wisdom: Invest in the market. Get someone you trust. Don't let fear stop you. Get comfy being uncomfortable. It brings courage. I once took on a business client that was so huge a company for me, that after I took them on, I felt like throwing up each morning preparing for the project. I knew I had to "bring it"! To get everything in place and to get it in place now! Even though I was scared to death, I still did it! And I learned and proved to myself that I could do it, and I grew immensely from the experience.

Connie's Insights: While Wendy did not have a role model, you can see that she became one. And not just for women in her line of business, but for people in any line of business. She was taught scarcity, but she changed that thinking as she grew and has an abundance mindset now. It didn't come without stretching outside of her comfort zone. She faced fear and conquered it, and that helped build more confidence.

DONNA CORLEY

Age: 49

Current Position: Strategic Advisor, Board Member, Public Speaker, Board Member for PennyMac Mortgage Investment Trust Holdings, LLC, Founder and CEO of Guiding Star Advisory, LLC, Board Member, Bite Me Cancer Foundation, Formerly EVP and Head of Single-Family Business for Freddie Mac.

Q: What's most important to you about money?

A: I retired from Freddie Mac as one of the most senior executives there. I worked my way up from being an analyst who started the day after my college graduation 27 years earlier. I have two teenage kids to help through college. We tell them to investigate scholarships, and we started the 529 plan (college funding plan) for each of them when they were born. So much of their college is hopefully taken care of. When I started with Freddie Mac, I maxed out my contribution to the 401K. Each time I received a raise, I increased the contribution by that amount. I was already used to living on a certain amount, so it made sense to me to increase savings for retirement. I have an amazing partner who has flexibility in his work, and he was the primary care giver for our kids while I worked crazy hours. The most important thing to me about money is that it provided all these things for my family.

Q: What is your next big goal? What's the next level for you?
A: I have two big goals: The first is to get the kids through college. Second, since I am retired now and at an early age, I am toying around with the idea of working on corporate boards and to be able to work at something fun at my leisure.

Q: What does life look like in the future? Can you paint the picture for me?
A: We live in Washington DC during the school year and at our house on a lake in Maine during the summer. We love it there. Once the kids are done with school, we plan to spend six months in Maine, and each year we would like to pick a different place to explore and vacation. A house in Italy or Australia might be nice—somewhere international.

Q: Have you ever worked with a financial advisor/planner before?
A: Yes. While I have my CFA designation that makes me qualified to do my own investing, I didn't have enough time to do it well. In 2005, we started using my in-law's advisor. We have that level of trust baked in because of that family referral. Freddie Mac had rules that I could not invest myself without clearing it with the company, so I left it to our advisor.

Q: What do you love best about working with them?
A: The level of trust that we feel with him. He has our best interest at heart. He has frequently given advice that we know has not made him any money personally. He helps us accomplish our goals.

LET'S TALK ABOUT SOME CHALLENGES, FEARS, AND FRUSTRATIONS.

Q: What is the biggest thing holding you back or slowing you down from reaching your goal(s)?
A: The stock market performance, inflation, and the housing market.

Q: What's your number one concern?
A: It's important that my kids develop a strong work ethic and financial acumen. I wonder if I do enough to encourage it, like my parents did for me.

Q: What do you know now that you wish you would have known early on?
A: Recognize that every decision you make should be the best for where you are right now in life. Three months from now it might be a different one.

Donna's Words of Wisdom: Have money to be able to be smart with. It starts with money coming in. Especially for women: know your worth and make the money that you deserve!

Connie's Insights: Donna is an inspiration. She's totally living the dream! I love how she shared that each time she got a raise, she would increase her retirement savings by the amount of the raise and continued to live on what she was used to living on. This alone, in my opinion, is part of what catapulted her to be able to retire so early. She worked hard, was smart with her money, and has been blessed with a financial advisor she can trust.

CHRISTINA THOMAS-LEWIN, FCMA, CGMA, BA (HONS) ODCP

Age: 39

Current Position: Chartered Global Management
Accountant, Organizational Development
Certified Professional and Interior Designer

Christina is an educated woman. She and her husband (the CEO
and president of his company), both come from humble beginnings
in social housing where they grew up in England. She grew up with
two working parents. Her dad was a firefighter and provided lawn
care services in their local village. Her parents divorced when she was
five. Her mom was a hairdresser and cleaned the local library to make
ends meet. The clothes she wore were mainly hand-me-downs from
her sister or knitted sweaters from her grandma. Together, they now
earn over six figures annually.

Q: What's most important to you about money?
A: It allows me to forever help our family at home in England—our
children, grandchildren, and siblings, as well as my mom and dad.
Right now, in England, gas and electric are increasingly expensive.
And food is quite costly as well.

Q: What do you really want that you don't have right now?

A: I am not big into material things. I love being able to help my family. My husband and I love simple things: giving to our family, being able to enjoy going to dinners with each other, etc. Even having a pool is a blessing to us. It is something I never would have imagined ever having when I was growing up.

Q: What's your next big goal; what's the next level for you?

A: I would love to be the corporate controller at my company, hopefully in five years or so down the road. Presently, I love the team I work with, and I want to keep building them up by training and helping them to be self-sufficient and their best selves so that they can go forward and make a huge impact.

Q: Have you ever worked with a financial advisor?

A: Although I am certified substantially with my accounting background, my expertise is in corporate management. I look at income, balance sheet, and cash flows for my company. My husband and I work with a CPA right now, who does audit and tax consulting for us. I love that our CPA has the specialized knowledge for the US tax returns, and that helps us greatly.

Q: What's the biggest thing holding you back or slowing you down from reaching your goals?
A: I would love to get my PhD in the US, and the conversion process from my studies in England to the US is slowing me down. I would already have had my PhD in England, but I must take a master's class here in the US to convert the classes I have taken, and that is pretty frustrating for me, but I am working on it.

Q: What do you know now that you wish you would have known early on?
A: I've always wanted to make sure that after bills are paid, we could live comfortably and support others.

Christina's Words of Wisdom: Success to me is finding more joy from helping others along the way.

Connie's Insights: Christina and her husband, despite their modest beginnings, refused to let life's limitations define them. Their story is a testament to the power of courage and perseverance. They achieved remarkable success through sheer determination and hard work, and their genuine kindness serves as a beacon of inspiration. Their journey is not just about financial success but about the uplifting human spirit that drives them to greatness.

KIM HARRINGTON

Age: 47

Current Position: Managing Member, Ambrose Properties, New England, LLC

Q: What's most important to you about money?
A: Money is a means to an end. My view has shifted from focusing on making money to focusing on finding ways to add value. This brings more joy and less stress. I'm a pretty faith-filled person, and I have felt God's call to really focus on adding value to others' lives through my work.

Q: What do you really want that you don't have right now?
A: I don't want a lot materialistically. I want to make an impact on my community and society. I want to build up my kids and their generation, to understand their gifts and help them contribute to society in positive ways.

Q: What's your next big goal? What's the next level for you?
A: I want to amass more assets that appreciate—specifically rental properties, apartment buildings, and commercial properties.

Q: What do your finances look like in the future? Can you paint the picture for me?

A: I will continue to purchase investment properties. In five years, I'd like to have three more apartment buildings and be at a point where I won't have to build houses to maintain income. I think long-term wealth is built by owning investment properties that cashflow and appreciate over time.

Q: If you could wave a magic wand, what does life look like for you?

A: Besides my real estate business, I also enjoy working with my husband and his team at Sharpen Skills Training LLC. He is creating an impactful business within mental sports performance by carving a niche supporting athletes and teams to grow stronger in the mental side of their sport. We built an athletic training facility a couple of years ago and have found that athletes not only need to hone their physical abilities, but they also need to focus on their mental strength. Kids are struggling with anxiety and all kinds of issues these days, but there is a stigma to getting the help they need. We want to help break that barrier by focusing on mental sports performance skills that these athletes can then take into every aspect of their lives.

Q: Have you ever worked with a financial advisor/planner before?

A: Yes, I find value in diversifying my investments and not focusing solely on real estate, although I do love real estate!

Q: **What do you like best about working with your financial advisor?**

A: She seems to think of *everything*! I like her philosophy of putting the right assets into the right buckets based upon my risk tolerance and long-term plans. I also love that she helps me focus on how I can attract and retain the best employees by helping us manage a SIMPLE IRA. She provides advice on succession planning and business insurance needs to protect me and my family. I highly recommend working with someone who has really studied investment concepts and opportunities that you haven't. Let's be real. We can't be experts at everything, so find an advisor who is passionate about what they do so you can focus on what you do best.

LET'S TALK ABOUT SOME CHALLENGES, FEARS, AND FRUSTRATIONS.

Q: **What's the biggest thing holding you back or slowing you down from reaching your goal(s)?**

A: I believe things will always go wrong. Knowing what's in your control and what's not in your control is key.

Q: **What challenge do you have that you would love to be solved right now?**

A: There is a business relationship that I need to get out of.

Q: What do you know now that you wish you would have known early on?

A: The different structures for different partnerships. I gave too much away in the beginning years. You can't win if you don't have equal power. I wish I had stronger negotiation skills when I first started, and then I'd be in a better position.

Kim's Words of Wisdom: You are here for a reason. Figure it out and do it by surrounding yourself with the right people. Also, I strongly believe that you should absolutely have some long-term investment in real estate. Real estate should be part of a strong portfolio.

Connie's Insights: Kim is impressive in the real estate industry and is a strong role model for women wanting to get into that market. I agree with her that having real estate in your portfolio along with stock market investments is a sound strategy that gives you diversification. And she's certainly on to something with their mental health program for young athletes, too.

DR. KIMBERLY SAMAHA, PHD

Current Position: CEO at Synthesis Venture Partners,
CEO at Born Global Foundation, US and Europe.

She specializes in the deregulated energy market and integrating start-up ventures into large multi-national corporations. She founded several international forums to foster dialogue and collaboration among stakeholders in the energy and ethics domains.

Q: What's most important to you about money?
A: We should call it currency. I don't think money flows correctly. It depends on your intention with it. If the intention is greed, then I believe it's dirty. Money is not static. They say if you have it, you are a winner, but it depends on where it flows. It can create pathways for impact. I like to realign the intention from static to flowing into good things that provide good opportunities to helping people.

Q: What do you really want that you don't have right now?
A: To activate heart centeredness, living our daily lives in true alignment with our values and purpose.

Q: What's your next big goal? What's the next level for you?
A: I'd like to experience heart centeredness myself—to be peaceful in my integrity, to live up to my core values.

Q: What do your finances look like in the future? Can you paint the picture for me?

A: My finances are very good. I have money and influence.

Q: If you could wave a magic wand, what does life look like for you?

A: I'd like to give the audience a different light. If you can get people to turn their head away from darkness, from things like pornography and give little points of light they can turn to, even for just a moment, that would be great. And then do that again and again.

Q: Have you ever worked with a financial advisor/planner before?

A: Since we are an international family company that operates on three different continents, we always have financial advisors and lawyers we turn to for advice. My goal is to live smaller. I think about how the extra money should flow, where it should go to best make an impact.

LET'S TALK ABOUT SOME CHALLENGES, FEARS, AND FRUSTRATIONS.

Q: What is the biggest thing holding you back or slowing you down from reaching your goal(s)?

A: I would like to have my foundation create employment and systems. I self-funded the foundation to date, and my biggest challenge is that I'd really like these projects to become self- generating.

We are bringing some projects to construction level. That was my hope, and now it's happening. It's wonderful for me to see it. Regarding bigger goals, I am in the legacy stage of managing now; I want to see things get built and running and creating because I believe this is my mission. So right now, I need to create these physical places where that can occur.

Q: What's your number one concern?
A: The systems themselves. It's a numbers game, and trying to raise money to fund it is real work. We're trying to create abundance and hope, but communicating that to our donors is rather difficult.

Dr. Samaha's Words of Wisdom: If you feel like this is the thing that God is calling you to, step out in faith and know that God will lead you. Also know that He will lead you back if it wasn't the direction He wanted you to go in. There is an authenticity to doing that.

Connie's Insights: I am grateful and honored that Dr. Samaha took time with me for this interview. It's not something she typically does. Her financial advisors have helped her make sound choices. Now with her influence she seeks to do greater good for the world through her foundations. I think her views provide food for thought on how we can think about money and the flow of it.

MICHAEL STONKUS

Age: 42

Current Position: IT Manager

Q: What's most important to you about money?
A: I think money provides stability. I have enough that I would be just fine for five years if I lost my job or something happened to me. I have a good chunk in cash as well as my 401k, and for fun, I follow the crypto market and invest some there.

Q: What do you really want that you don't have right now?
A: I am focused right now on being kind and doing good things for people who don't have much. The only thing I would really like might be a pontoon boat.

Q: What's your next big goal? What's the next level for you?
A: My next goal is to sit on a board and to lead people. Maybe a nonprofit and then move up from there.

Q: What do your finances look like in the future? Can you paint the picture for me?
A: My definition of wealth is to be able to afford the things I want. In a year, that could look like an upgrade to my savings and crypto

accounts. In ten years, I'd like to look at my accounts and see a robust 401k and investment portfolio and know that my income stream is better than today. In twenty years, I'd like to be able to work because I want to, not because I have to. I enjoy working, so I think I will always work. Being able to stop for a couple more rounds of golf during the week would be ideal.

Q: If you could wave a magic wand, what does life look like for you?
A: I'd probably have mounds of cash so that I never have to worry, and my daughter would not have to worry. I love spending time with my daughter, who is now ten. I am divorced from her mom, and that is not easy for my daughter. But I always make myself available for her.

Q: Have you ever worked with a financial advisor/planner before?
A: No.

Q: What do you think you might like best about working with them?
A: The insight they have for how to get the best investments and make them grow. And I'd like regular meetings to keep tabs on things.

LET'S TALK ABOUT SOME CHALLENGES, FEARS, AND FRUSTRATIONS.

Q: What's the biggest thing holding you back or slowing you down from reaching your goals?

A: I don't like debt. I have a mortgage and a car payment, and that is enough debt for me. Paying them off is a goal. As far as the pontoon boat, well, I could honestly probably just go buy it, but I love my cash. If I got a bonus or came into money somehow, I would go get it.

Q: What challenge would you love to be solved right now?

A: Fitness. I'd like to take more time to stay fit.

Q: Are there any areas where you feel like you are not capitalizing on all opportunities or leaving money on the table?

A: I think it's a good idea for me to utilize investment advice better. I'd like to see a financial plan for myself.

Q: What do you know now that you wish you would have known early on?

A: I had a lot of anxiety when I was young. It's rough, but the anxiety that you feel will lessen with time.

Michael's Words of Wisdom: Be kind. Everyone is carrying a cross to bear.

Connie's Insights: Mike brings a wonderful perspective and a common-sense approach to wealth. I admire that. He has some ideal thoughts and perspectives, like having a mound of cash available for opportunities or emergencies and having a sound investment portfolio. Also, he believes it's important to know what really matters to you and not to be afraid to seek out good advice. His number one concern is to be kind. That says a lot about him.

ANGIE DIANETTI

Age: 61

Current position: President and Visionary, Radcom

Q: What's the most important thing to you about money?
A: Money is a tool that makes dreams happen. You can go on vacations and pay for school. Money can buy experiences like Disney or whatever you choose to do for fun and enjoyment. It can also provide the means for me to invest in my business.

Q: What do you want that you don't have right now?
A: I would love to be able to travel more.

Q: What's your big goal? What's the next level for you?
A: Right now, I am developing intellectual property that is the toolkit for integrated performance which consists of a Role Overview and Output Files. By developing this into intellectual property, I will create a saleable business. I started the project three or four years ago.

Q: What would be the most ideal situation for you right now?
A: Right now, I would love to travel. I recently spent two weeks in Cancun. Half of the day I worked, and half of the day I played. It was perfect.

Q: Have you ever worked with a financial advisor?

A: We have worked with many financial advisors over the years. My husband is the one who takes the lead with them. He will usually have a reason to move to the next one—and the next— because he isn't happy with what they provide.

Q: What do you like best about working with a financial advisor?

A: My husband would like a financial advisor who pays attention to details. For him, there is no room for mistakes. Markets go up quickly, and they can come down quickly. We were in the process of selling his mother's house. His mom was working with an advisor then. That advisor never reinvested her earnings into the market to get an upside return. Instead, the returns went into a cash account. In doing that, the money did not grow as well as it could have, and I was very disappointed about that.

Q: What else would you like from your financial advisor that would make your experience more valuable?

A: I would like someone to keep in touch when necessary and be able to advise us as to what changes to make for what the market is doing. I would like someone who doesn't make him feel inadequate or unknowledgeable.

LET'S TALK ABOUT SOME CHALLENGES, FEARS, AND FRUSTRATIONS.

Q: What's your number one concern right now?

A: My concerns are not typical of most people. I am not worried about our decisions and plans or my capabilities of success but about the uncontrollable things that happen in political realms which can alter things for us. From my standpoint, I feel that certain political situations could result in the potential derailment of the work I am involved in.

Q: What do you know now that you wish you would have known early on?

A: That you should always be living in an abundance mindset. It's critical. It's the best way to generate more money. When you have a scarcity mentality, that puts you in fear of doing anything mode. And that's not good.

Angie's Words of Wisdom: Don't be afraid to do what you need to do to enhance your business. I had two clients who were high maintenance for the value that they brought us. I fired both as our two biggest clients. The result was that we doubled in size. So, two of my biggest clients were taking a lot of time and a lot of manpower. When I had the courage to fire them, our business doubled!

Connie's Insights: Angie is developing intellectual property so her company can be saleable down the road. This is the way she is choosing to fund a nice retirement. She knows the action steps that need to be in place to get it done and is implementing them.

NEXT, LET ME TAKE A MOMENT to share my personal journey with money—how my experiences from childhood to becoming a financial planner have shaped my approach to financial empowerment. And you'll be interested in some myths and truths about women and money.

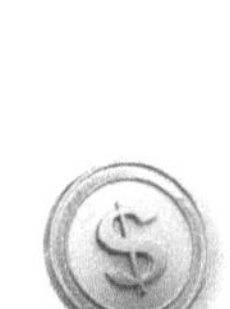

CHAPTER 2

Money and Me

Teach her about how money really
works, and she can change the world!

—Warren Buffet

FROM MY CHILDHOOD TO MARRIAGE

I grew up in a big family with my mom, dad, and six brothers and sisters. I'm the second oldest. Our house was always chaotic, but we had great fun. When I was growing up, our house wasn't filled with lavish possessions, yet we always had what we needed. I'm sure raising seven children posed financial challenges; however, we never knew about them. Mom and Dad didn't talk about money. I do have great memories of going shopping with Mom, especially for new school clothes and supplies—even on a budget. And Dad made sure we could enjoy our much-anticipated Saturday night dinners at the local steakhouse. Money and material things in our home weren't the most important. Consequently, without much dialogue on financial matters, we didn't learn about saving, investing, and future planning. However, what we did glean were invaluable life lessons centered on love of God, kindness toward each other, honesty, integrity, and the importance of family support and always thinking of and being there for others.

Fast forward a bit. I got married to a wonderful man, and we had four children. My husband has always been good with money—maybe to a fault. He's the frugal one in our relationship. I say that with a smile because I think opposites attract. I'm not a big spender, but I believe it's important to enjoy our life's journey. I think we've struck a good balance. We worked hard to teach our children the valuable principles of living a good life and caring for others first and foremost. Of course, we've also taught them sound money principles based on saving, investing, and putting away for the future. You'd expect nothing less from a financial planner, right?

FROM ENTREPRENEUR TO FINANCIAL PLANNER

In 1999, I embarked on an entrepreneurial journey by founding my own residential mortgage company, which flourished for a remarkable thirteen years. However, the unforeseen market downturn in 2008 brought about a significant setback. The recession abruptly halted the flow of business to my company as the demand for home purchases and refinancing plummeted. This downturn had a profound impact on my income. It was a period of harsh lessons learned: I realized I lacked sufficient capital to sustain my business through tough times, and I held onto employees longer than I should have, exacerbating my financial situation. Regrettably, these choices plunged me into considerable debt. While I'm admittedly embarrassed by these missteps, I share my experience so others can take away valuable insights. This challenging period underscored the importance of maintaining a robust savings account—sufficient funds set aside to weather any unforeseen storms in life. The future is unpredictable; hence, the necessity of being prepared.

After a short stint in the banking industry, following that experience, I delved into the realms of investing and financial planning, driven by a curiosity about my own retirement alongside my husband. I wanted to know that we would be prepared. While we had a vision for our retirement lifestyle, we recognized the importance of asking critical questions: Did we have adequate savings to retire on our terms, or would we be compelled to prolong our working years beyond what we wanted? What strategies could we implement to transform our dreams into reality? Was an adjustment to our savings plan or lifestyle necessary?

As a financial planner, I have acquired a wealth of valuable knowledge and insight and successfully applied it to our own lives resulting in profound satisfaction for both my husband and me. Witnessing the positive transformation, it brought about, I'm eager to extend this opportunity to others. Engaging in this process is not only enjoyable but also endlessly rewarding. It's a continuous journey ahead, where each step forward opens new possibilities.

As evident from my story, I persevered despite encountering setbacks like the aftermath of the mortgage business collapse during the 2008 Recession and the subsequent transition into a different financial domain. Life often presents challenging lessons, and I certainly made some mistakes. However, every obstacle is a valuable opportunity for growth. Isn't that the essence of life? We glean wisdom from our missteps, emerging wiser and more resilient through our unwavering determination to avoid repeating them.

Now, I pour my heart into my work, driven by a passion for supporting others, especially women. Why? Because I firmly believe there is power in financial planning, education, and the implementations of effective financial strategies. My goal is to empower individuals, enabling them to make sound choices and harness the potential of their money and what it can provide for them and the world. It's about creating a life that resonates with a future dream vision.

MY PASSION FOR EMPOWERING

Here are some reasons why I'm passionate about helping women (although I'm also passionate about helping men).

Facts that bother me—a lot:

As women, sometimes we've grown up and been fed lies about money from a young age. We've been told we're bad with money, we can be frivolous spenders, and we're incapable of investing or paying off debt.

Only 39% of women are confident they'll have enough resources to last 25+ years in retirement, according to Willis Towers Watson.[1]

Did you know that 90% of women feel they aren't making the best investment choices?[2] They still give that role to their husbands (which is fine for some), but if they don't have the confidence they can do it, that's not fine!

Is it because women lack role models? Could be. But in this book, you'll discover many who are role models. They're the smart, talented women I interviewed for this book.

More facts that provide opportunity for change:

- Fewer than 70% of women are saving for retirement.[3]
- Some women don't want to climb the corporate ladder, and that's okay. If they have zero interest in climbing ladders or being a leader, we need to respect that. Some just want a fair wage that allows them to live comfortably without stress. But we should encourage the women who want to be leaders if that's their goal. Economists say over the next twenty-five years, there will be a Great Wealth Transfer. Approximately $68 trillion will change hands from older generations to younger.[4]
- By 2030, women are predicted to control two-thirds of private capital.[5]
- Today, women control one-third of total US household financial assets—more than $10 trillion.[6]
- Roughly 70 percent of US affluent-household investable assets are controlled by baby boomers. Two-thirds of baby-boomer assets are currently held by joint households where a female is present but not actively involved in financial decisions.[7]

- As men pass, they will leave control of these assets to their female spouses, who tend to be both younger and longer lived. In the United States, women outlive men by an average of five years.[8]

A potential wealth transfer of such magnitude means we must teach our women how to best invest and be confident in their ability to make not just *good*, but *great* money choices, including how to protect it. This can happen if we educate and teach young girls by sharing successes and failures and inspiring them.

One of the reasons I wrote this book is to connect and empower you, my readers. I hope the book brings out the best in you and those I interviewed in an authentic way.

"IF YOU COULD SNAP YOUR FINGERS and change one thing right now, what would it be?" Todd Henry asks this in his book *Die Empty*, and I ask you a similar question.

If you could snap your fingers and be *financially free*, would you do that?

I believe in you, and I believe you can! You wouldn't have picked up this book if you weren't curious about making smart money choices. And you wouldn't have read this far. I believe you can do great things, create the life you want, and axpand your vision for the future.

You already have good things in place. Let's expand them. But before we talk about basic aspects of money—financial planning, investing, life insurance, and annuities, let's take in the next set of interviews. They reveal powerful stories and strategies that can transform the way you think about your own financial future. Get ready to be engaged. These insights aren't just inspiring; they describe actionable options, offering fresh perspectives to elevate your journey to financial success.

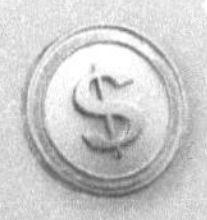

PERSONAL MONEY STORIES PART 2

RACHEL SHEPARD

Age: 41

Current Position: Founder LonaRock, LLC, Executive Chairman and CEO, LonaRock Capital Group, Executive Chairman and CIO, Fractional CFO

Q: What's most important to you about money?
A: The financial independence that it provides. Money provides stability and the feeling of peace. When you have enough of it, it means you don't have to worry about how you will provide for the family. It enables you to give back as well, and that is important.

Q: What do you really want that you don't have right now?
A: I am currently working on creating multiple streams of income. My consulting firm is one of those streams. Dividends from stock provide income as well. I believe owning real estate and other businesses would be a great diversifier for income stream strategies. I hope to own both someday.

Q: What is your next big goal? What's the next level for you?
A: Honestly, the big goal is to increase cash flow streams. I am working on a project right now that eventually could be a big deal for me.

Q: What do your finances look like in the future? Can you paint the picture for me?

A: In one year I will have grown the business and income streams. In ten years, I will still be in the accumulating phase, and I'd like to be in a position that we continue to grow.

Q: If you could wave a magic wand, what does life look like for you?

A: I would like for the business to be financially independent. I don't want to worry about paychecks coming in. It just takes time. I know it will come.

Q: Have you ever worked with a financial advisor/planner before?

A: Yes, I work with an online investment company.

Q: What do you like best about working with them?

A: I like the reporting that they provide for my investments.

Q: What else would you like from them that would make your experience even more valuable?

A: It would be ideal for them to bring up things like where I can be saving more or what other tools/products are available that would benefit me. I like the idea of a partnership with the person I work with and that they might be my greatest cheerleader. (I love this too. We all need a cheerleader and someone who can keep us inspired! – Connie's 2 cents.) That person I can count on to see the things that I may not see in my financial profile and tell me what I don't know.

LET'S TALK ABOUT SOME CHALLENGES, FEARS, AND FRUSTRATIONS.

Q: What is the biggest thing holding you back or slowing you down from reaching your goal(s)?

A: The number one thing is time. Taking time for my family is so important. There are certain things that money can't buy. Sacrificing financially is okay because family is more important to me right now. It's hard to launch a business or two and to be a good wife and mother as well. There are only so many hours in the day.

Q: What do you know now that you wish you would have known early on?

A: I always assumed that as a career woman, my income would keep increasing. I wish I knew that you must pivot from time to time. With family for example. I would have had that cash cushion. I used to use shopping as therapy, so I spent instead of saved.

Rachel's Words of Wisdom: Have a producer mindset instead of a consumer mindset. For instance, when we "consume" Netflix or video games, or whatever, we are sitting around "doing" instead of "creating." Go and create something! Look for ways to grow, create, save, and give. Be creators of those things that you love.

Connie's Insights: Rachel is succeeding in helping many of her clients make it to the next level because of her expertise. Her words of wisdom are inspiring as well.

DYLANI HERATH

Age: 44

Current Position: FinTech Leader, VP of Engineering, CHIEF member, TechStars Mentor, Awarded Top 25 Women in FinTech

Q: What's most important to you about money?
A: I am very fortunate. I came from parents who were financially sound. I am married with three children, ages 26, 14 and 7. I am financially free and financially stable. Money is used for saving, investing, spending, and charitable causes. I am from Asia (Sri Lanka). In Sri Lanka, we have deep rooted economic accountability, where I learned that you don't buy things on credit or use loans. I was taught not to use credit because it creates debt. Money brings independence and provides identity.

Q: What do you really want that you don't have right now?
A: I came to the United States for my career. I was born in Sri Lanka. I plan how to spend my money. But what I really want is family members around me. I miss that tremendously.

Q: What's your next big goal? What's the next level for you?
A: I want to continue to impact people and communities around me. I want to be someone my children are proud of. I am honored to be

able to serve in the FinTech industry and community, to deliver, reach and create accessibility for minority and underserved communities to access and maintain financial wellbeing.

Q: What do your finances look like in the future? Can you paint the picture for me?

A: I can easily retire in ten years, but I will always work in some capacity. I like to look at individual investments and am interested in areas, such as real estate, private equity, and energy tech.

Q: What would be the most ideal situation for you right now? If you could wave a magic wand, what does life look like for you?

A: I have all that I need. I would love for my kids to have a solid education and the support needed to be independent.

Q: Have you ever worked with a financial advisor/planner before?

A: I do my own investing for a portion of my income. However, we also have a financial advisor who manages our portfolio. We like that— to ensure clarity for our future.

Q: What do you love best about working with them?

A: I do like that we don't have to keep up with the market ourselves. I like the expert advice and getting updates on overall trends. I do not have time to study or research. I have trust that our advisor does what's best for us.

Q: **What else would you like from them that would make your experience even more valuable?**
A: I don't like to worry about the taxes. My husband takes care of that with our tax advisor. I also like that my husband takes care of our bills as well.

LET'S TALK ABOUT SOME CHALLENGES, FEARS, AND FRUSTRATIONS.

Q: **What is the biggest thing holding you back or slowing you down from reaching your goal of making an impact?**
A: The uncertainty in the market, of course, slows me down from reaching monetary goals. Also, I give my time and talent to charitable causes when I can, although my work slows me down from doing it more.

Q: **What challenge would you love to be solved right now?**
A: I would like to invest in real estate. My husband is conservative right now though, so it's just not a good time yet.

Q: **What worries you?**
A: I worry about my kids not having enough family around. I worry about my family.

Dylani's Words of Wisdom: I would tell my younger self to start investing young—digitally and traditionally in the stock market. Invest in real estate and have property. Build savings.

Connie's Insights: Dylani is straightforward in her approach, knows what she wants, and has a quiet confidence in her abilities. While she has a drive to do more, she remains humble. This is honorable indeed.

ELIZABETH BROWN

Age: 29

Current Position: Associate Attorney for Business and Real Estate and part of the firm's Business Department and Real Estate Practice Group.

Q: What's most important to you about money?
A: Money is a tool. Money gives you the freedom to have more time and the opportunity to invest in the things you enjoy and to give back to the community. It can be used for different goals. It provides security and freedom.

Q: What do you really want that you don't have right now?
A: I am very interested in community development and real estate. I like the idea of preserving older buildings and restoring them so that they can have a new purpose in and for the community.

Q: What's your next big goal? What's the next level for you?
A: I may pursue becoming a partner. My skill set is growing with a passion for real-estate. An intermediate step is I'd like to purchase a building on my own or with my husband and brother.

Q: What do your finances look like in the future? Can you paint the picture for me?

A: In one year, I don't see much of a change in lifestyle. We like to go out to eat a lot, but I am cognizant of saving money so that I have a substantial amount in savings. In ten years, I would hope to own a couple of historical buildings that I could work on to revitalize communities.

Q: If you could wave a magic wand, what does life look like for you?

A: All things considered, my life is pretty great, but I'd love more free time. I want to get rid of my student loan debt, and I'm grateful for the scholarships that helped me get through school.

Q: Have you ever worked with a financial advisor/planner before?

A: No. My husband has a finance background, so he has knowledge and a skillset to manage our money, although we both make all our big financial decisions together.

Q: What do you think you might like best about working with a financial advisor?

A: The expertise they bring about the stock market and market trends—what is and isn't working. They spend their time staying on top of that so that you don't have to.

LET'S TALK ABOUT SOME CHALLENGES, FEARS, AND FRUSTRATIONS.

Q: What's the biggest thing holding you back or slowing you down from reaching your goals?

A: Simply the timing of my husband and me pursuing investments at the same time. He's in the trenches of building a young company, and I would like to buy historic buildings. Both are good for both of us, but he started pursuing his goal first, so it's wise to get it stable before I pursue mine. He supported me early in our relationship and during law school, so I appreciate the opportunity to be the breadwinner now, and I will be able to pursue my goals soon. He also supports me being the breadwinner. I think this is a good thing for your readers too, especially for young women to see this as a healthy dynamic.

Q: What challenge do you have that you would love to be solved right now?

A: Decision paralysis. Sometimes "analysis paralysis" takes hold and keeps you from deciding which road to pursue next.

Q: What do you know now that you wish you would have known early on?

A: I have always been good about saving. I wish I knew better what to do with my money. I know I should talk to an advisor.

Elizabeth's Words of Wisdom: Remember that money is a tool. Don't be consumed by it. Good habits lead to good things. Don't be consumed by consumerism.

Connie's Insights: I appreciate that Elizabeth has a healthy perspective of money—not to be consumed by it, but to have good habits around it.

RICHARD SMITH

Current Position: Innovation & Strategy, Project Management, Leading Cross Functional Teams, Signet & Signet Jewelers

Q: What's most important to you about money?
A: Money provides security. Knowing that I have it so that if something comes up, I don't have to worry too much. I had a lot of student loan debt I would love to be rid of. When I was growing up, there were three children in a family of five—a typical middle-class family. We were frugal. If we went out to eat, we all got water because not getting the drinks allowed us to go out more. We were taught to appreciate money. Once, my brothers and I all wanted a Nintendo. We saved our money and pitched in to get it. We all had skin in the game, so we learned to appreciate things.

Q: What do you really want that you don't have right now?
A: A bigger house. My wife and I are happy. We have three young kids—6, 5, and 1. We could use an extra bathroom! [He said laughing].

Q: What's your next big goal? What's the next level for you?
A: I'd like to put more money into investing, but I think we need the bigger house a little more right now. We are sacrificing to make that happen. My wife works part-time right now too to help us get it.

Q: What do your finances look like in the future? Can you paint the picture for me?

A: In one year, I don't think things will look much different. Two family members gave us a gift of stock, so maybe we can use that for part of a down payment on a new house. In ten years, we hope to be living more comfortably, have a nice size emergency fund, and do more active investing.

Q: If you could wave a magic wand, what does life look like for you?

A: Three things: 1) I'd have a lot of money in the bank as my emergency fund, 2) My investments would be making money, 3) We'd have our dream house and be saving for college for the kids.

Q: Have you ever worked with a financial advisor/planner before?

A: No, but I see the value in it. When I can, I'll have one. I'm very interested in what they might do for me.

Q: What else would you like from them that would make your experience even more valuable?

A: I see them providing education on investment strategies and what the right strategies would be for my wife and me in investing and building our wealth.

LET'S TALK ABOUT SOME CHALLENGES, FEARS, AND FRUSTRATIONS.

Q: What is the biggest thing holding you back or slowing you down from reaching your goal(s)?
A: More money. We have a budget, and we prioritize. The new house is where the money goes right now. When we have enough, we'll buy the bigger house.

Q: What challenge do you have that you would love to be solved right now?
A: My student loan debt to be paid off. I only have a very small amount left to pay it off completely.

Q: What do you know now that you wish you would have known early on?
A: That the cost of student loans is substantial. Pay attention and take out as little as you can because you must pay it back with interest. It will slow you way down in accomplishing other things early in your career if you have a lot of it. So be careful about what you are spending.

Richard's Words of Wisdom: Get comfortable with understanding your money—what you can and cannot do with it. There are repercussions for what you spend.

Connie's Insights: Rich brings up an important point when he talked about saving up for a Nintendo. When they got it, it was like gold for them. It's good *not* to give our kids everything, although we are tempted to. It's good to teach them to save and buy their own things occasionally. This does more than just create good money management skills; it creates a discipline toward money and a healthy view of it. It also creates personal pride. They set a goal and work to achieve it.

RENEE

Age: 36

Current Position: Petroleum Industry
Professional, Investor, Business Owner

Q: What's most important to you about money?
A: Money brings independence and stability. I want independence as a woman, and I don't want to rely on anyone else. I love my husband very much, but I am also independent.

Q: What do you really want that you don't have right now?
A: I'd like to retire from my corporate job.

Q: What's your next big goal? What's the next level for you?
A: To retire from corporate America. I could retire right now with income from other entrepreneurial endeavors. I don't like to rely on just one source of income, so I diversify between stock market investments, real estate, and my day job. They will all serve as income later.

Q: What do your finances look like in the future? Can you paint the picture for me?
A: My net worth is over $2 million right now, and my husband has money on top of that. I would like to get that to the $5 million mark,

and I'd be able to live off the interest. I have an LLC and buy real estate properties and rent them out in Ohio and South Carolina. If I want to retire at age 45 or 50, I know that I can. I have a 401k and a pension. I also have a Roth IRA that I contributed the max to prior to reaching the income limit.

Q: What would be the most ideal situation for you right now? If you could wave a magic wand, what does life look like for you?

A: I'd like to have more investment properties. I'd like to get my Chartered Financial Analyst (CFA) designation.

Q: Have you ever worked with a financial advisor/planner before?

A: We work with an advisor through a work provided 401k. I'd like to work with a personal financial advisor, but I haven't found one that's the right fit.

Q: What do you think you would love best about working with them?

A: Their expertise. I could rely on them because they work in it every day. It would be great to have someone keep an eye on things and advise accordingly.

Q: What else would you like from them that would make your experience even more valuable?

A: Planning and risk management in general. And to adjust the risk management as we go. I would gladly pay a fee for that.

LET'S TALK ABOUT SOME CHALLENGES, FEARS, AND FRUSTRATIONS.

Q: What is the biggest thing holding you back or slowing you down from reaching your goal(s)?
A: Inflation. Housing is expensive, and interest rates are high, and I am waiting for the right time to add to my portfolio. Healthcare insurance is a concern as well. I currently use my employer benefits for my family.

Q: Are there any areas where you feel like you might not be capitalizing on all opportunities or leaving money on the table?
A: I have a lot of cash that I should have invested.

Q: What do you know now that you wish you would have known early on?
A: Don't rely on corporate America. I thought I was going to work hard and move up the ladder, but this did not work out as I anticipated. You almost must choose between your personal life and your career. I would recommend having an entrepreneurial mindset and diversity early on with your own business and investments as well.

Renee's Words of Wisdom: Don't spend more than you make. Don't spend it before it's in your hand. Take full advantage of your employer's 401k match and save/invest as much as possible early on.

Connie's Insights: Renee is impressive! She is a strong, confident woman. She has a matter-of-fact attitude, she knows what her goals are, and she is working to get to where she is going. Her focus is what makes her a role model for anyone wanting to follow in her path.

TRINITY GERMAIN

Age: 54

Current Position: Director, Leadership
Development, nonprofit organization

Q: What's most important to you about money?
A: Money creates financial freedom. I've always been kind of conservative and a saver. I don't get down when the market goes down. I don't worry because I know it will come back around.

Q: What do you really want that you don't have right now?
A: To retire early. You never know what life is going to bring, and I want to enjoy life with my family. There's no guarantee that you will be here tomorrow. I just lost my brother. He was sick for a while and then spent some time in hospice. Losing someone you love is one of the most difficult things to go through, so you look at life through a different lens because of it.

Q: What's your next big goal? What's the next level for you?
A: I'd like to live in Arizona or the Carolinas. I'm taking a real estate investing class. Getting into investment ownership could be the next level for me. Owning a home in Arizona or the Carolinas (or both) and renting it out when we are not there would be fun and a good investment.

Q: What do you expect your wealth to look like in the future?
A: All my money is in the market right now, and it's done well. I think that will continue.

In ten years, I expect I will be retired. I have kids who are 18 and 22. One of them is graduating from college, and one is just starting college. We pay for that, but that expense should be gone in ten years.

Q: Have you ever worked with a financial planner?
A: Yes, for 7-8 years now. I've only been married to my husband since 2018. Prior to that, I've been on my own, and it was important for me to have somebody I could trust and who would guide me to good financial decisions. We do quarterly check-ins. We talk about certain things, and he does some education with me. Even with all I've learned, I still don't feel 100% confident with all there is to know about investing and financial planning.

Q: What would make that partnership more valuable?
A: More education. I would love if they had workshops I could go to.

LET'S TALK ABOUT CHALLENGES, FEARS, AND FRUSTRATIONS.

Q: What's the biggest thing that's holding you back or slowing you down from reaching your goals?
A: Insurance and health benefits slow me down from retiring sooner. It's so expensive to pay for those on your own. When you work for a nonprofit, you don't get insurance benefits.

Q: What challenge would you love to be solved right now?
A: Taxes. Reducing my tax liability. I don't think I am capitalizing on tax write offs. I pay a boatload in taxes. I'm trying to find ways to reduce my tax liability. I've done well on the stock market, and because of that, my tax liability is high.

Q: What do you know now that you wish you would have known earlier on?
A: Three things: 1) It is wise to keep things separate from your spouse. You never know what can go wrong. 2) Keep tabs on your credit. You don't realize how important it is until you don't have it. 3) Finally, start saving early in life.

Connie's Insights: Trinity obviously has a good understanding of financial planning and the importance of it. It can help take her to the next level in her wealth. However, there is so much to know. I like that she's hungry for the education about her investments.

KEVIN

Age: 50

Current Position: Director of Marketing and Operations for a consumer products company

Q: What's most important to you about money?
A: Money gives you the ability to have freedom for decisions both personally and professionally. It can improve your life by helping you be prepared for what it brings you.

Q: What do you really want that you don't have right now?
A: I rent right now, and I would like to buy investment property. I want to partner with someone and be able to have more control about where I am headed financially. I have stock and other investments currently, but I think it is smart to be more diverse. Owning real estate can bring that diversity.

Q: What's your next big goal? What's the next level for you?
A: I am growing in my career. I offer legal and/or financial advice for large corporations. I'd like to create more of a passive income stream for myself. I'm working on that as well.

Q: What do your finances look like in the future? Can you paint the picture for me?
A: Because I am 50 right now, I'd like to max out what I contribute currently for my retirement in the 401k. In ten years, I'd like to be able to have the full freedom to consider retiring. I might continue to work professionally and build my financial investments, but it would be great to have the possibility of retirement available.

Q: If you could wave a magic wand, what does life look like for you?
A: I'd like to be in a position where I have options—to enjoy life and to help my family. My dad died recently, and I'd like to support my family as much as I can.

Q: Have you ever worked with a financial advisor/planner before?
A: Yes. I work with the advisor that provides our 401k. I have some money in mutual funds, and I like index funds too.

Q: What do you like best about working with them?
A: I like to use them as a sounding board. They give me validation for what I am doing. Sometimes they have new ideas for me as well.

Q: What else would you like from them that would make your experience even more valuable?
A: The biggest disconnect is that there is a void in tax and investment planning. I need sound advice for the tax planning piece. I think it's super important for an advisor to talk about end of life and wealth preservation too.

Q: What's the biggest thing holding you back or slowing you down from reaching your goal(s)?
A: Time. I need more time to devote to real estate and family responsibilities.

Q: What's your number one concern?
A: Right now, my dad just died. My brother is the trustee of an irrevocable trust, and that is a lot to get through.

Q: What challenge would you love to be solved right now?
A: I am the CFO to help my mom through the loss of my dad.

Q: What do you know now that you wish you would have known early on?
A: I wish I would have known about compounding interest and the power of it. As you age, you learn and see how important that is.

Kevin's Words of Wisdom: Learn about compound interest! Make sound judgments and be risk balanced. Have some money handy so that you can capitalize on new opportunities that present themselves. Do your research. If it seems good, take the risk.

Connie's Insights: I really like Kevin's perspective on the importance of getting sound advice about your money. If you are a widow or widower left to assume the responsibility of managing the money but don't know the ins and outs of the household finances, it does take some adjusting. And in this case, it is a blessing that Kevin is available for his mom and family.

ALECIA BAKER

Age: 58

Current Position: Director of Community
Relations for a large city school district

Q: What's most important to you about money?
A: Money provides security. It allows you to do what you want when you want. It's important to keep in mind that you need to save to provide security later in life as well.

Q: What do you really want that you don't have right now?
A: I feel like I have enough. My children are going to college and will graduate with no debt. I feel fortunate that I can help with their education. It's great to have money, but I think time is the bigger asset. The more time you have, the more you can enjoy experiences.

Q: What's your next big goal? What's the next level for you?
A: To retire—but not from work. I would like to start a personal training program or maybe teach yoga. I would enjoy that immensely.

Q: What do your finances look like in the future? Can you paint the picture for me?
A: Hopefully, my finances look better and continue to grow in one

year from now. In ten years, I can start taking from my savings and retirement and enjoy experiences.

Q: If you could wave a magic wand, what does life look like for you?

A: To maintain where I am now. I'd like to take a deep dive into what I will do after I retire and to give that some thought. I'd like unlimited time—time to myself, not to have to report to a job. I'd like to travel and enjoy meaningful experiences with my daughters.

Q: Have you ever worked with a financial advisor/planner before?

A: Yes. We have had a relationship with a financial advisor for many years as well as a good accountant. I have not done any estate planning yet but should probably do that soon as well.

Q: What do you love best about working with them?

A: I like the history we have together. Historically, we have done better than the S & P index. He is savvy about which investments are doing well and which are not, and I like the constant communication. Typically, we talk by phone and discuss any tax implications.

LET'S TALK ABOUT SOME CHALLENGES, FEARS, AND FRUSTRATIONS.

Q: What's the biggest thing holding you back or slowing you down from reaching your goal(s)?
A: The stock market right now. I have a pension through my work, but the market is not doing well over the past couple of years, so it's a matter of persevering through it.

Q: What's your number one concern?
A: I don't want to outlive my money. I also want to know that my family will be taken care of.

Q: What do you know now that you wish you would have known early on?
A: I wish I had started to save sooner.

Alecia's Words of Wisdom: If you want financial security later in life, start to save and build your nest egg sooner.

Connie's Insights: I like Alecia's perspective that time is more valuable than money. We only have so much of it and are never certain how long we have, so it is super important to enjoy life and the people in it. In her mind, to enjoy experiences is to live well. And I agree.

As we move forward, we'll delve into your personal goals and craft a strategy that paves the way for enduring prosperity. Financial planning is where we start.

CHAPTER 3

From Planning to Prosperity

A goal without a plan is just a wish.

—Antoine de Saint-Exupéry

I SAY THE WAY TO ACCOMPLISH your goals is through careful financial planning. I can't speak for all financial planners because we each have our own way of planning and serving our clients, but here's what I think is important about it:

DEFINITION OF FINANCIAL PLANNING

Financial planning is the art of helping you create, manage, and optimize your money to achieve the financial life you want. It involves a holistic assessment of your finances—basically everything involving your money:

- liquid assets such as checking and savings accounts
- investments
- retirement plans like your 401k and current pensions
- real estate that you own
- current and future tax implications specific to you
- insurance policies
- estate plans

Once you take a step back and look at all of that, you can create an effective financial plan that helps to protect all the positive things you have going on and serves to increase your wealth by optimizing your money and adding new investment strategies if necessary. Your plan can help you get to your short- and long-term goals faster. This is so important!

Look, we don't know what we don't know, and working with a financial planner and implementing strategies you may not know about could exponentially make a major difference and impact your life significantly.

MY APPROACH TO FINANCIAL PLANNING

I enjoy working with people who are eager to see their money grow and reach its full potential. We talk about your goals, and I encourage you to dream a little. What could you do to create joy in your life now? What do you want your future to look like? Is there anything you want to avoid? Let's solve for that. Is there anything that you fear?

Let's solve for that. What are some challenges and frustrations you've run into so far? Let's solve for that, too.

I specialize in providing investment guidance and education geared towards achieving your financial goals. My approach prioritizes discussing the results that various strategies can create for you rather than focusing solely on the specific products themselves. It's what they can do for you that matters most.

Ultimately, what's most important is the success and progress you can achieve through implementing these strategies, regardless of the tools or products involved. My expertise in the tools can help provide the specific results you are looking for.

Investment options encompass a range of strategies tailored to your risk tolerance, spanning from more aggressive to conservative approaches in the stock market. Additionally, you may consider incorporating life insurance, annuities, or other complimentary strategies to align with your financial objectives. And we talk through all of that because the options can seem complex. My approach is to simplify it so you can understand everything.

When you take the time to prepare and plan, you gain clarity on the vision for your future, and you will know exactly what steps to take to realize that vision. Remember Abraham Lincoln's quote at the beginning of Chapter 1? It is worth repeating. He said, "The best way to predict the future is to create it." Absolutely! I believe the best way to create security and financial independence is by financial planning.

To simplify it:

Step 1: Think about your goals—short and long-term. Create your vision for financial wealth. What does it look like for you?

Step 2: Identify what is holding you back or slowing you down from that vision.

Step 3: Talk to an expert. Seek out a financial advisor and discuss.

Step 4: Let them help you create the plan and then work it.

The advantages of having a financial plan and working with a financial planner become evident when you can visualize your future on paper. There is something about seeing it on paper too, a graph showing you exactly where you are. You can assess whether you are on track or facing any shortfalls. You will also gain insights into your projected social security benefits and estimates for your own 401k or pension income. And together, we can plan for tax strategies that may benefit you.

If you are doing just fine, don't you want to know that now? If you're short, don't you want to know that now, as well? Small changes can make a significant difference.

THE POWER OF FINANCIAL PLANNING

Some of the women (and a few men) I interviewed for this book admitted they just don't have time to manage their money—or even want to. They lead such hectic lives, and the pressures of everyday life make it almost impossible to even think about good money strategies. They believe they can easily share their goals with their financial advisor and leave it to them to manage their money for them.

I say, bravo! It's such a relief to have someone you can trust and depend on to lead you to a desirable future and grow your wealth financially.

I want to emphasize though, the importance of always knowing what your money is doing and where it's going. Yes, you can hire someone who is trustworthy to help and can take care of most matters for you, but you should always be involved at some level—eyes wide open. **No one will take care of your money like you will.** Never be afraid to ask your advisor about the whats and the whys of your investments and their recommendations. That goes for the gains and losses as well. If your advisor is honest, they will be transparent with you.

Always know where your money is and what it's doing.

Warren Buffet says, "Risk comes from not knowing what you are doing." Most financial advisors do what they do to help you manage that risk.

It's essential to work with someone you can trust and who has your best interest at heart. Of course, you want to work with someone who's good at what they do. So how do you know if the financial planner you're working with— or thinking about working with— is the right one for you?

What people seek in a financial advisor is not just competence but care. They don't want to feel like just another account or part of a client base. They expect, as they should, a high standard of service. I believe that's the baseline. What truly matters is offering personalized attention, where clients are remembered and valued throughout their journey. Beyond building financial security, people want to create a portfolio of experiences, knowing they are in a meaningful, trusting relationship. That's the level of connection and commitment I strive to provide.

WHAT TO LOOK FOR IN A FINANCIAL ADVISOR

What are their core values? Do they have integrity? Are they a fiduciary? Are they honest? Are they trustworthy? Have they been highly recommended by someone you know who works with them?

Look for someone you like. You will be sharing with them extremely personal information, and it's important to be comfortable working together. The fact is you're probably going to deal with them for a long time. They might just become a devoted friend.

Look for someone who will give you personalized attention and an elevated experience. If that's important to you, make sure they will.

Look for someone who will tell you the good and the bad. They should be honest, transparent, and comfortable telling you "like it is." Let's face it! When it comes to the investment piece of your portfolio, the situation will not always be rosy. The market goes up and down. They need to tell you the truth about that.

Look for someone who talks to you about your risk tolerance and takes that seriously. If they are talking you into more aggressive investment choices than you are comfortable with, they may not be a good fit for you.

Talk to them about their investment strategy. Do they like long-term investing, or are they more short-term day trader types? Which one resonates better with you? Choose that one. A financial advisor should be able to *educate you* about why they are investing in certain products for you. For example, are they using Exchange Traded Funds (ETF's) or mutual funds? Why? Are they investing in individual stocks. Why? Make sure you agree with their suggestions.

Are they a holistic planning advisor? Do they look at the whole picture, or do they only deal in life insurance and annuity products, or only in investments and the stock market? Is it important that you find someone who is well-rounded and provides well-rounded advice? Seek them out. If not, that's okay, too. I know many advisors who are experts in a particular area.

You can also check advisors out on FINRA's
(Financial Industry Regulatory Authority)
BrokerCheck website. https://brokercheck.finra.org/

As we draw this chapter to a close, I hope it's clear that effective financial planning is not just about the numbers; it's about building a secure foundation for your dreams and aspirations with someone you like and trust. A skilled financial planner serves as both architect and ally, helping you construct a roadmap to navigate life's financial challenges with confidence and clarity. By entrusting your financial future to a trusted advisor, you're not merely seeking guidance; you're investing in peace of mind, knowing your goals are within reach. As you embark on this journey towards financial well-being, remember the transformative power of expert guidance and its profound impact on your life. The possibilities are endless. I admire your desire to improve your life.

LET ME SHARE A LITTLE STORY.

Kelli, a successful executive, was juggling multiple responsibilities at work and home. Amidst her busy schedule, she found time to talk to a girlfriend who shared that she had just worked with a financial planner and was excited about her money and future. Kelli realized she had neglected her own personal finances. Feeling overwhelmed, she decided to seek the guidance of a financial planner herself.

She searched on LinkedIn to find someone who resonated with her—someone who was actively posting and competent, yet empathetic and seemed to have a heart to make an impact. Kelli felt sure she had chosen just the right one after she interviewed her and felt they clicked. Together, they meticulously crafted a comprehensive plan tailored to Kelli's goals and aspirations.

Through diligent planning and strategic decision-making, Kelli not only gained clarity on her financial situation but also discovered opportunities for growth and security. With her advisor's assistance, she optimized her investment portfolio, minimized tax liabilities, and established a robust retirement plan.

As a result of her proactive approach to financial planning, Kelli experienced a newfound sense of confidence and control over her financial future. Thanks to the guidance of her financial planner, she no longer felt burdened by uncertainty but instead embraced each day with a clear roadmap towards her long-term goals.

This is just one of many stories I could tell you about one approach to finding a financial advisor.

NOW, LET'S TURN TO THE THIRD SET of interviews, where—among eight stories, we describe a successful woman who had it all together but then had to deplete her life savings because life can sometimes throw us a major curve. Fortunately, she is overcoming the obstacle and saving again. Her story and other conversations you're about to read will inspire you to think bigger and push the boundaries of what's possible in your financial journey.

PERSONAL MONEY STORIES PART 3

ASIA WINTERS

Age: 45

Current Position: Managing Director, Accounting, Certified Intel Analyst at Business Intel Company

Asia has a strong ability to strategize and increase a company's profitability and is highly regarded for her track record of process development and redesigning for growth.

Q: What's most important to you about money?
A: Security. I'm single. I don't want to "just get by!" I work hard and have given up a lot, so I want what I have saved so far to count. Being able to take care of myself and having enough money to be stable is important to me. I like to spend money on my nieces and others, and taking care of my mom and helping the community is important.

Q: Is there anything you really want that you don't have right now?
A: I would love to do a great job of investing. I contribute to my 401k and Roth account within it. But I have been saving for thirty years and still wonder if it's enough or as much as it should be.

Q: What does life look like one year from now and ten years from now?

A: In the last 2 ½ years, I had to deplete my savings. Life sometimes throws you challenges, so now I need to focus on building that again so that I have my "emergency fund." That's my one-year goal. In ten years, I want my savings and investments to have grown and compounded significantly higher than they are now.

Q: If you could wave a magic wand, what does life look like?

A: I would love not to be in a state of always pulling money out of my savings. I would love *not* to have the discomfort of things not going as planned. I don't feel secure right now. If I had more money in my savings, I would feel a lot better. In the last couple of years, I have had a ton of expenditures. I had two homes in Boston. I sold both and kept the one I had in Cape Cod. I moved to Ohio to take care of family in 2021.

Q: Have you ever worked with a financial advisor?

A: Yes. Years ago, I had one in Cincinnati, OH. I have one now, and I have had her for about six years.

Q: What do you love best about working with her?

A: She is honest and candid and does tax harvesting for me. She helped direct me to set up a will and long-term insurance.

**Q: What else would you like from your financial advisor
that would make your experience even more valuable?**

A: I would like her to be more active during the year and put things
in writing. I want to know my level of taking risk in the market is ok.
I want to know I have enough money to do everything I want to do
and not run out of money!

LET'S TALK ABOUT SOME CHALLENGES, FEARS, AND FRUSTRATIONS.

**Q: What's the biggest thing holding you back or slowing you
down from reaching your goal?**

A: My biggest worry is about outside issues I don't have control of,
such as job loss or not staying at a certain pay scale. I worry about
expenses going up and unexpected family issues. Any short or long-
term emergency depletes my savings.

**Q: What do you know now that you wish you would have
known earlier on?**

A: Investing more in my 401k and investing more outside of that
too. I wish I knew to keep an eye on my money and made changes
if it wasn't growing as I thought it should be. They say, "Do this!" or
"Invest this way!" but that might not have been right for me.

Asia's Words of Wisdom: We can all save for our retirements. Money isn't always the problem. Knowledge can help us. Don't let fear be the biggest factor and keep you from investing in yourself.

Connie's Insights: Asia is wise and good with her money. Her priority to take care of herself and be able to give to others is inspiring. Her story also shows us that you can be brilliant, but it doesn't mean major challenges won't arise that need to be dealt with. Some circumstances can completely deplete what we thought was a good savings plan.

THORA REIKER

Age: 55

Current Position: Board Director,
International Business Executive

Q. What's most important to you about money?
A: 1) Money provides security for the future and gives you the ability to take care of your family, 2) Money provides a comfortable lifestyle.

Q: What do you really want that you don't have right now?
A: I am retired as an executive at Microsoft and now serve on several boards at a professional and consulting level. I love knowledge, and learning is something I constantly seek.

Q: What's your next big goal? What's the next level for you?
A: I am defining that right now. I am making some income and finding more flexibility in life. My husband and I feel very blessed to be at this point in our lives.

Q: What do your finances look like in the future? Can you paint the picture for me?

A: In one year, I will still be making an income, but more important to me is making an impact. In ten years, I will be providing safety and security for my children in the future.

Q: If you could wave a magic wand, what does life look like for you?

A: I love my career serving on company boards right now, and I take on advisory roles with them. Two are private, and three are publicly traded. I have also been on a nonprofit board, and we donate to those because that is important to us. Exercise and keeping fit, time with family and friends—and for myself—are priorities.

Q: Have you ever worked with a financial advisor before?

A: Yes. They help balance our portfolio and manage risk. We are not aggressive in the market and our investments. I also like real estate.

Q: What do you love best about working with them?

A: I like that they are trustworthy and proactive. When things change, they reach out to us and provide true guidance. They make investments that make an increase over time. Our financial advisor is very savvy in international tax guidance. I like having access to experts internationally for tax purposes.

LET'S TALK ABOUT SOME CHALLENGES, FEARS, AND FRUSTRATIONS.

Q: What's the biggest thing holding you back or slowing you down from reaching your goal(s)?
A: There are things that you can't control like deteriorating health, and that's ok. You never know.

Q: What's your number one concern?
A: Making sure that my children are okay. I feel good about the choices my husband and I have made so far.

Q: What challenge would you love to be solved right now?
A: Climate change concerns me. I would love people to spend more effort solving it. Practical things will solve themselves, so I don't worry too much about them. I have a husband I rely on and get plenty of support from him.

Q: What do you know now that you wish you would have known early on?
A: How cyclical life is—that things that worry me today will be different than things that worry me next year.

Thora's Words of Wisdom: Not everyone will have the same opportunity to plan like I did, but to the extent you can, please do that.

Connie's Insights: Thora is confident because she has provided financial security for her family, and it has allowed for flexibility in the next chapters of her life. She has made smart decisions, and that is what has gotten her to where she is today.

KRISTIN EVANS

Age: 42

Current Position: VP of Marketing at SSP, an oil
and energy company in Twinsburg, OH.

Q: What's most important to you about money?
A: The most important thing about money is the security it can bring.
I'm single, and I want to be able to take care of myself— always. I
never want anyone to have to take care of me. I have nieces and nephews I love, but I sure don't want them to have the burden of taking
care of me later in life. When you have money, you have options.

Q: What do you really want that you don't have right now?
A: More time to travel. I travel all over the world for my company and
have been to many places, and I am grateful for that opportunity. But
when I travel for the company, there's no time to enjoy the experience
of being there on a personal level.

Q: What's your next big goal? What's the next level for you?
A: Deciding the direction of the company. Instead of being primarily "transactional" in bringing on new clients, I want us to be more
"intentional" in bringing on new clients. Choosing ideal clients for
the company would enable exponential growth.

Q: What do you want life to look like in the future. Can you paint the picture for me?

A: One year from now I want to be financially set. I want to continue being responsible with my money and have the money situation intact. I was never taught how to do financial planning. I've always known that savings is important, and I've saved. I'm just not sure my money is working for me as hard as it should be. In ten years, I want to be confident that I will have optimized everything I'm doing with my money and feel very secure about my future.

Q: If you could wave a magic wand, what would life look like right now?

A: I would have enough money to carry me through whatever life brings and never be caught off guard.

Q: Have you ever worked with a financial planner?

A: I have never worked with a financial planner. I feel insecure about not being knowledgeable about financial planning and how to make the most of my money and savings, so I feel somewhat inadequate, so I'm nervous to ask anyone for help. It would be so helpful though, to have someone look at what I have and guide me about what changes I should make, if any—someone to help me optimize the money I have now and walk with me into the future with recommendations.

LET'S CHAT ABOUT SOME CHALLENGES, FEARS, AND FRUSTRATIONS.

Q: What's the biggest thing holding you back or slowing you down from reaching your goals?

A: Not knowing who to reach out to and feeling inadequate around money slows me down. I'm concerned that with inflation, and so many other matters, something might happen that could derail my financial plans and future goals.

Q: What's your number one concern right now?

A: I don't want to leave money on the table, so to speak. I don't think I'm optimizing all that I have financially.

Q: What challenge do you have that you would love to be solved right now?

A: Because of COVID-19, I have the challenge to source raw material right now. And another challenge is hiring good labor.

Q: What do you know now that you wished you would have known earlier on?

A: I feel lucky because I learned early that saving more than you spend is very important. When I was in college paying for an apartment and making just enough to pay the bills, it dawned on me, if I would have saved when I didn't need to (earlier on) then I could have been able to buy what I wanted— like clothes, fun stuff, and going out.

Kristin's Words of Wisdom: Ask. Because you don't know what you don't know. Seek out a financial advisor.

Connie's Insights: Kristin is very educated and sensible and could recognize that she had cash in places that weren't being optimized. You will be happy to know that since this interview, Kristin does have a financial advisor and is optimizing everything she has for her financial future.

JANET KENDALL WHITE

Current Position: Founder and CEO, Berkshire Group, Inc. Authorized Partner and Certified Facilitator Everything DiSC, The Five Behaviors.

Q: What's most important to you about money?
A: I think money provides freedom—freedom to choose to travel, drive the kind of car I want, live where I want to live, and not be a burden on anyone as I age. Freedom though, is much bigger than the monetary things that money can buy. Freedom is being able to live the life you choose, one of joy and faith. To be wealthy spiritually in that regard is everything.

Q: What is it that you really want that you don't have right now?
A: I would like to decrease my credit line because business has been much better now after surviving COVID-19. I would love to travel to Italy and Ireland. I'd like to buy a house very soon as well.

Q: What is your next big goal? What's the next level for you?
A: My next big goal is for business growth. I would like to double my revenue. I am developing a product to bring to market in book form. I think that will be a great enhancement to how we provide our services.

Q: **What do your finances look like in the future? Can you paint the picture for me?**

A: Within a year, I want to get rid of debt I took on because of COVID-19. Second, I'd like to increase my investment portfolio. Third, I will have acquired a good down payment for the new house. In less than five years from now, I'd like to be able to do what I want, when I want, and with whom I want. I would also like to be able to have my business in a place where my daughter can take it over if she chooses to.

Q: **If you could wave a magic wand, what does life look like for you?**

A: I don't think life would be much different. I feel blessed. I ask myself who is God putting in my life that I can share Him with, and how can I let my light shine. I also want to be continually supporting other women business owners regularly and impact the ecosystem that we operate in.

Q: **Have you ever worked with a financial advisor/planner before?**

A: Yes, I have a financial advisor and an accountant.

Q: **What do you love best about working with them?**

A: I have worked with my CPA for a long time. He understands my business, and there is no fuss or muss. Same with my financial advisor; I understand her, and she is easy to work with. She gives good advice and has helped me through a couple difficult situations.

LET'S TALK ABOUT SOME CHALLENGES, FEARS, AND FRUSTRATIONS.

Q: What's the biggest thing holding you back or slowing you down from reaching your goal(s)?
A: The biggest thing holding me back from buying a new home is the market for homes right now.

Q: What do you know now that you wish you would have known early on?
A: I look at it this way: If I had changed anything, I may not have learned (albeit the hard way) the lessons given to me. I got the knowledge by going through it. For instance, at one point I had a client who held a lot of weight in my business portfolio, and the contract ended successfully, but that left a huge hole in revenue. That taught me not to allow it to happen again. Another piece of advice might be that if I had hired a CPA five years earlier than I did, I likely would have made different and possibly smarter choices.

Janet's Words of Wisdom: Always have good advisors on all fronts. Be clear that their values and principles are like your own. Surround yourself with a network of like-minded people who will take you to where you want to go and not hang out with those who would keep you where you are.

Connie's Insights: Janet knows her goals and works her plan. She knows that having good advisors is key, understanding that her knowledge and expertise can only take her so far.

LISA MALLIS

Age: 50

Current Position: Founder, Impactive Strategies, LLC, Delegate Like a Pro

Q: What's most important to you about money?
A: Money allows me the freedom to do what I want without having to worry about how to pay for it.

Q: What do you really want that you don't have right now?
A: My husband retired in 2022, so I would like to have a larger nest egg so that I can pay for my own health insurance. He has insurance, but if/when I retire, I will have to provide for that.

Q: What's your next big goal? What's the next level for you?
A: I am creating an on-demand time management program so I can have passive income and won't have to work as much. My goal is to have a hybrid system in place where there is some face-to-face, and I can work with VIP clients. One of my clients gave me the idea. She came to one of my trainings and wanted the same training for her employees. But she had no way to get them there physically. She told me "If you build it, I will buy it."

Q: What do your finances look like in the future? Can you paint the picture for me?

A: In one year, my program would be launched, and that should take care of the health insurance problem. In ten years, I should have enough residual income coming from my products to be able to vacation more and do what we want to do.

Q: If you could wave a magic wand, what would life look like for you?

A: I would have the ability to work with exactly the type of clients that I love to work with! I'd work three days a week, and we would travel more. I'd like to do fun stuff like rent a house on the ocean and vacation there. We are big on family vacations. We have three children with five grandchildren we like to vacation with, so it would be a dream to be able to do that when we want to.

Q. Have you ever worked with a financial advisor/planner before?

A: Yes.

Q: What do you love best about working with them?

A: We work with my husband's pension guy. I like that he reached out to us when COVID-19 hit and said, "Don't freak out! We planned for this, so don't worry. You have your retirement for a reason." He's always been calm and proactive amid storms. That has helped us to be less stressful and to know that things are going to be okay. I also have a great accountant who isn't afraid to speak with my advisor, so I like that a lot.

LET'S TALK ABOUT SOME CHALLENGES, FEARS, AND FRUSTRATIONS.

Q: What's the biggest thing holding you back or slowing you down from reaching your goal(s)?

A: I need one more person to add to my team so I can free up more of my own time to complete the on-demand project I am working on.

Q: What do you know now that you wish you would have known early on?

A: I grew up valuing hard work, but I've learned that there are ways to demonstrate your worth beyond relentless grind and overtime. Discovering the right path, the perfect fit activity, is more impactful than tackling a list of tasks. It's about quality over quantity; achieving the right things matters more—doing that one thing perfectly. This mindset shift can lead to a shorter workday. It may provide the way to a five or six-hour workday for you instead of eight to ten hours a day.

Lisa's Words of Wisdom: Today is the best day to start! If you see something in this book that you think is a good idea, do it today, not when "things slow down."

Connie's Insights: Lisa has a vision for her future and is working to accomplish it. One of her major concerns is being able to afford healthcare, one of the biggest worries for most Americans. For those nearing retirement, many will choose to postpone it because they aren't confident they can afford health insurance before Medicare kicks in at age 65. This is one area where financial planning can help. I love her words of wisdom too!

PHIL SOENCKSEN

Age: 55

Current Position: Award Winning Senior Writer, Marketing Communications at Kent State University

Q: What's most important to you about money?
A: Money is terrifying. The most important thing to me is to never run out of it. I am married with no children, and I need sustainability. Besides my OPERS that I pay into from Kent State, I had an inheritance, and I keep contributing to it.

Q: What do you really want that you don't have right now?
A: I would like complete assurance of my ability to retire and to know when and if I can.

Q: What do your finances look like in the future? Can you paint the picture for me?
A: In one year, I don't see much change. I am very conservative in my investment choices. In ten years, I will be 65. I will hopefully retire at age 62.

Q: If you could wave a magic wand, what does life look like for you?

A: Right now, my wife and I live separately because of our jobs. She lives in Illinois. She is retired now and leads a team at a software company. I would love to live with my wife in Illinois. We have been married fifteen years and see each other once a month. I would like to work in a library or history museum as a volunteer or curator when I retire.

Q: Have you ever worked with a financial advisor before?

A: Yes. Several of them. I don't like working with them, though. Right now, I am currently only working with the provider of my pension plan, and it's going well. In 1990, I had a 401k and moved it to an IRA with a financial advisor. I lost half of what I put in there. I *hate* losing, so everything I have now is in conservative funds.

Q: What else would you like from them that would make your experience even more valuable?

A: Concrete answers. I'd like a presentation and a financial plan. I'd like to know more about the WEF (Windfall Elimination Provision). I'd like to know what my paycheck will be at retirement.

(WEF affects social security retirement and is complex, so we are unable to go into depth to explain here.)

LET'S TALK ABOUT SOME CHALLENGES, FEARS, AND FRUSTRATIONS.

Q: What's the biggest thing holding you back or slowing you down from reaching your goal(s)?
A: My age. I am only 55 now. I can retire in seven years.

Q: What one challenge do you have that you would love for it to be solved right now?
A: No flexibility to work remotely. I would love to be able to work remotely.

Q: Are there any areas where you feel like you might not be capitalizing on all opportunities or leaving money on the table?
A: I wonder if I should be a little more aggressive. Maybe I should, but I don't trust the market. I want certainty.

Phil's Words of Wisdom: Start saving early. It's hard because you are usually not making a lot of money when you start, but at least do something to save. Think about a financial plan when you're younger. Don't count on your company to provide all your retirement. Keep working and don't take a break.

Connie's Insights: Phil is the first interviewee to tell me that he didn't like working with a financial advisor. I respect his honesty. He did not have a good experience; he lost half the money he put into his account with them. You can see why money is terrifying to him.

I can completely understand. While it is likely, and quite normal, to lose some and win some (so to speak) in the stock market, it's essential to have an advisor who listens to you and who will recommend investments according to your risk tolerance and what you are comfortable with. There are strategies for the certainty he needs. A financial advisor would give him clarity about his financial future and identify shortcomings if he has them.

PATRICIA MERCER

Age: 60

Current Position: Management Consultant,
Executive Coach

Q: What's most important to you about money?
A: Security. The way I feel about money is tied up with how I grew up and what our parents taught us about money. I don't need luxury and don't feel I need to leave the kids with millions of dollars. I feel it's important to have the security and comfortability that money brings. My husband loves to handle the money. He's done well in the market, sometimes by a little bit and sometimes by a lot. At one point, I was a stay-at-home mom. When I went back to work, my primary goal with my business was to provide tuition for our two boys at private schools and college. I paid for all their college. I have three semesters left. We didn't set up a college fund; we did a pay as you go month by month.

Q: What do you really want that you don't have right now?
A: More hours in the day.

Q: What is your next big goal? What's the next level for you?

A: We bought a new house a year ago and are working on updating it for the future. It's a fun major project. My next business goal is to build the business that is relatively new where we bring on more partners and junior consultants and really build a firm. Also, I feel volunteering is super important; serving on two boards keeps me busy.

Q: What do your finances look like in the future? Can you paint the picture for me?

A: In one year, I think we will be about where we are today financially. We expect a huge outflow with the house renovation—then a big inflow with my husband's sale of one company. In ten years, we'll be socking away for what people call retirement. We don't really think of "retirement" though. We are happy with what we do and will continue if we can.

Q: If you could wave a magic wand, what does life look like for you?

A: We can always use more money, but I feel like we have everything we need and everything we want. That is a *huge* comfort. We can do good now for others as well. There were times I thought of buying a summer house on the lake in Michigan, but we looked, and it just isn't that important anymore. My husband travels a lot, so when he comes home, he just wants to be home. We own a home in Ireland with my brothers and sisters that we can visit whenever we want. I think over the years that dreams change, and we are just loving life as it is and spending the money as we see is good for us.

Q: Have you ever worked with a financial advisor/planner before?

A: My husband has worked with someone for twenty-five years. I'm not excluded, but I'm not involved. And that is okay with me. I trust my husband to take care of it. He's the expert, and I let him do it.

LET'S TALK ABOUT SOME CHALLENGES, FEARS, AND FRUSTRATIONS.

Q: What's the biggest thing holding you back or slowing you down from reaching your goal(s)?

A: For the goal of growing the company, it's time. There are not enough hours in the day. The balance between serving my current clients and planning for the future is strenuous.

Q: What do you know now that you wish you would have known early on?

A: How brutally expensive college is. I probably should have been putting money away early on. But I think the way that we did it worked, and I'm very proud of that!

Patricia's Words of Wisdom: Understand—and really know—the dollars coming in and the dollars going out. Keeping track of the money is especially important for people who are not on a payroll. You must keep track of revenue and expenses.

Connie's Insights: I like the comment that "dreams change," and they changed their goals as the years passed. Transitions happen in life for all of us, and what might have been important ten years ago may not be as important as we grow.

ANAMARIA

Age: 47

Current Position: Social Worker and Judicial Psychology,
Assistant Director at a nonprofit agency

Q: What's most important to you about money?
A: Safety. To have enough that will cover your basic needs. I see single moms working so hard to make ends meet.

Q: What do you really want that you don't have right now?
A: I would like the ability to travel around the world and within the United States. I am not able to do that as much as I would like to.

Q: What's your next big goal? What's the next level for you?
A: I would love to go back to Europe. I am from Romania, but some of my family is in England, and family is of huge importance to me. I want to give my daughter the joy of being surrounded by family. She is 8½ now. My husband's mom and dad are here in the US, so that is a blessing, but they are not healthy.

Q: What do your finances look like in the future? Can you paint the picture for me?
A: In one year, I see us still being here with the family. I hope to

increase my income with my career, and my plans are to get a new job making more money.

Q: If you could wave a magic wand, what does life look like for you?

A: It's hard for me to dream because I am very practical and logical. I chose a career that doesn't provide a lot of money, but I am rewarded in other ways. I dream on a small scale because of where I am at. I would love for my daughter to have the freedom to make plans and travel without worrying about money. Her cousins are in London. I'd like her to be able to see different cultures too.

Q: Have you ever worked with a financial advisor/planner before?

A: I work with the people at my agency for my 401k. I put the maximum contribution in there, but no one helps me to decide exactly how to allocate it into the different investment choices. I think it would be a huge benefit if I had a financial advisor to help me.

LET'S TALK ABOUT SOME CHALLENGES, FEARS, AND FRUSTRATIONS.

Q: What's the biggest thing holding you back or slowing you down from reaching your goal(s)?

A: The first thing is money. The second thing is that I have limited vacation time compared to other countries who provide more vacation time for employees.

Q: What's your number one concern?
A: Missing out on family time. My mom is getting older. She is 67 and lives in Romania. My sister bought a house in Romania for all the family.

Q: What challenge do you have that you would love to be solved right now?
A: A license in social work is the ticket to more money for me. I must wait for my certificates to be approved in the US. That will take one year. Then I must take an exam. So, my goal to be able to make that happen is 1½ years.

Q: What do you know now that you wish you would have known early on?
A: Safe ways for taking risks on investing. I will come into an inheritance, so I need to figure out what I can do with that.

Anamaria's Words of Wisdom: I appreciate the opportunities that America gives to me. Being able to give my child a life would not have been possible in Romania. Being in America has also opened doors for me as well.

Connie's Insights: Anamaria's story is about coming to America and making a better life for herself, her husband, and their daughter. I am touched by the enormous amount of love she has for her family. She possesses such a precious heart and chooses a life where monetary things are not that important. Family is the most important thing to her. I love her perspective and her grateful heart.

NOW LET'S EXPLORE the world of investing—where strategy meets opportunity to help you build and grow your wealth.

CHAPTER 4

Risk, Reward, and Resilience: Investing to Grow Wealth

You have to keep learning if you want to become a great investor. When the world changes, you must change.

—CHARLIE MUNGER, WARREN BUFFET'S LONG-TIME PARTNER AND FRIEND.

IS INVESTING IN THE STOCK MARKET WORTH IT? YOU DECIDE.

What is investing? Investing is about taking calculated risks with your money to try to earn more with it. You buy an investment like a stock or bond hoping its value will increase over time.

A QUICK GLANCE AT THE HISTORY OF THE STOCK MARKET

Did you know the stock market originated outside the US? The stock market as we know it today started in Amsterdam when the Dutch East India Company became the first company to sell shares of its stock to the public. This allowed them to raise money, and in 1611, the Amsterdam stock exchange officially opened for business.[9]

Exchanges first began as moneylenders bought and sold debt. Eventually, trading evolved, and in 1790, the Philadelphia Stock Exchange became the first in the United States. As of 2024, the NYSE and Nasdaq are the biggest exchanges worldwide.[10] The stock market is a fundamental component of the global economy and an avenue for wealth creation and economic growth.

There's opportunity to begin modestly and achieve significant growth when you invest in the stock market, but there can be pitfalls along the way.

Why do people invest?

So they can potentially:

+ retire and have more income.

+ realize their dreams.

+ achieve financial freedom.

+ diversify their real estate portfolio (which is advisable)

+ take ownership of their future.

+ and maybe, most importantly, provide a legacy for their kids.

Investing is fantastic, but how do you know what to invest in?

I like to ask:

+ How do the wealthy of this world invest?

+ How would your portfolio look if you implemented some of their strategies?

+ How incredible would it be to have some of their knowledge?

What if you could partner with someone who ...

+ can help you implement some of those strategies? Or someone to educate you on stocks and bonds?

+ loves to keep up with the markets, does the research for you, and can recommend what to invest in that would suit you personally?

+ continually monitors what you are invested in and could suggest changes when appropriate?

Do only the wealthy have these kinds of partners? NO!
Is it possible to find a partner like this? YES, you can!

I've learned so many life lessons. One is that good money management can be a game-changer. Financial planners/advisors have studied savings strategies and how to use the stock market as an investing tool. Usually, by using various investing strategies, they apply them to their own retirement plan as well as for their own families, and they can do the same for you.

Financial planners are usually licensed with a Series 7 and 65 or 66 licenses and are trained, talented, and skilled at putting together investment portfolios. A candidate who passes a Series 7 exam is qualified for the solicitation to purchase and/or sale of all securities products. Series 65 and 66 are State licenses. Not all financial planners are created equal, but knowing they have this specific education is essential.

WHEN IT COMES TO INVESTING, BE WARY OF NEWS HEADLINES!

There's so much noise out there about investing. You must figure how to cut through the clutter and decide for yourself who to listen to. The media likes to make everything a bigger deal than it usually is, including the stock market. Find a source or someone you can trust who provides reliable information. That person could very well be your financial advisor.

Falling markets and dramatic headlines can tempt you to abandon your long-term investing strategy and take your money out of the market. You might think, let's wait until it's over, hoping to catch the market at its lowest point before you buy back in. Sometimes, in rising markets, you may seek to sell your holdings because you think it's at its peak.

Timing the market is essentially impossible, however, so remember to stick to your game plan. There's a reason you chose the investments you made. Only change if there is significant reason. And a talented financial advisor will help you do this.

When/if you pull out of the market, you will definitely seal the deal on any losses. History has shown that just a few trading days can be responsible for the largest gains during a recovery. **Being out of the market guarantees that you miss out on the most profitable periods.**

Don't get me wrong. I hate losing money. But if you start with wise investment choices, have healthy diversification, and only change things when necessary to minimize loss, that could be the best approach to investing.

Here are ways you can weather any storm:

Tune Out the Noise – Again, turning off the financial news station might be smart if it keeps you from making mistakes based on emotion.

Revisit your asset allocation – If you're near retirement or you just can't sleep at night because of the volatility in the market, it might be a good idea to rebalance your portfolio to something better suited to your comfort level. You can do that by working with your advisor. In fact, I make proactive phone calls to my clients to discuss their portfolios at least annually but usually more often. This way we keep up on the emotional and logical piece of investing.

Have realistic expectations for the market to begin with – US stock and bond markets have posted remarkable returns for the last few decades. You can develop a plan that will still achieve your goals despite the potential for up or down returns.

- **Always, always, always stay diversified** – There are at least eleven sectors in the market. Sectors are categories of companies that operate certain types of businesses. They are materials, industrials, financials, energy, consumer discretionary, information technology, utilities, communication services, health care, consumer staples, and real estate.

If one sector goes down in the market and you're heavily invested in that sector (say the tech sector), you will suffer greatly. The better way to invest is to be diversified in different sectors so that when one sector does poorly (which it will from time to time), your other sectors "balance" you, therefore blunting the impact. Your financial advisor can help you choose how to best diversify for your specific risk tolerance. This can put you on track to achieve your financial goals.

HERE'S A QUICK STORY.

A client called me and told me her son said that she should put all her assets into one stock. He was positive it would do well. She called me to talk about that. I told her what I will tell you: You should *never* put all your money into **one** investment unless you don't mind losing it all. Diversify. It's so important.

In closing this chapter, there's so much more to know regarding investment choices. It would take pages and pages to give you a complete education on it, but this chapter should get you started with the basics.

As we move into the middle of the book with the fourth set of interviews, you'll hear from individuals who have faced significant challenges and emerged stronger. Their experiences offer valuable lessons on resilience, determination, and the power of strategic planning

One compelling story recounts how she experienced a 20% loss in the stock market yet continues to uphold a commendable perspective on her investments. Many others express a lack of confidence in their investment knowledge, leading them to depend on their financial advisors for guidance and support in navigating the complexities of the market.

PERSONAL MONEY STORIES PART 4

BRIDGET RICHARD, LISW-S

Current Position: Founder Lamplight Counseling Services, LLC; Psychotherapist and Psychoeducational Trainer

Q: What's most important to you about money?
A: Having it! It is nice to have money. As a social worker, you don't make a lot of money, but there are other rewards, of course. Doing what I have done, owning several offices is not a bad way to go. I didn't have a scarcity mindset. I try to have an abundance mindset.

Q: What's your next big goal? What's the next level for you?
A: I want to be 100% debt free and have a fully funded retirement within one year.

Q: What do your finances look like in the future? Can you paint the picture for me?
A: I have been very blessed. It seems I have always been surrounded by good people. I am always in the right place at the right time, and I am grateful for that. My own relationship around money changed significantly when I became a business owner. I made myself change from a lack of money mindset to being comfortable with money and having it. I have been in business for nine years and for the first seven, each year it doubled.

Q: If you could wave a magic want, what does life look like for you?

A: To have a property near a ski resort. I'd also love a beach property. To be able to travel to Europe and do weekend trips with my husband would be amazing as well. We recently visited the Biltmore in Ashville, NC. I was able to participate in falconry for an afternoon, an absolute bucket list moment for me.

Q: Have you ever worked with a financial advisor/planner before?

A: Yes, I work with an investment banker. I started out giving him a certain amount per month to invest, and he doubled it. I think that if I stretch a little bit past my comfort zone in what I set aside with him, I'll get there. My husband is an IT Database engineer, and we both like to work with professionals outside our realm of expertise.

Q: What do you love best about working with them?

A: I feel encouraged and validated by him and the success I've had while investing.

Q: What else would you like from him that would make your experience even more valuable?

A: I'd like an understanding of how to possibly put money into other types of investments as well as education on what else is available to me.

Q: What do you know now that you wish you would have known early on?

A: Start investing early in life. I think of saving money early as habit building.

Bridget's Words of Wisdom: Don't buy into the hype of "You have to be a millionaire to be happy." Figure out what you want and how much it costs. Then figure out how to make it happen. It's as easy as that.

Connie's Insights: I admire Bridget for being extremely focused on each goal until she achieves it. It's not easy to stay on course when life comes at you, but she does it well.

KATHY DISE

Age: 71

Current Position: President,
BudgetEase Bookkeeping

Q: What's most important to you about money?
A: I like to put money on autopilot. Rules of thumb for me are: 10% to charity, 10% to 401k and pension, and have liquidity to buy into something when the time is right. I have been doing this for fifty years, and the results are good.

Q: What do you really want that you don't have right now?
A: A better stock market.

Q: What's your next big goal? What's the next level for you?
A: To provide a great work experience for my team that allows for work life balance, learning and growth opportunities. For my clients, my goal is seamless accounting support while enjoying interacting with their consultant.

Q: What do your finances look like in the future? Can you paint the picture for me?
A: This year, I have had a 20% loss in the stock market. I don't like

that. I'd like to work on a succession plan and put it in place so I can sell the business in ten years or less.

Q: If you could wave a magic wand, what does life look like for you?

A: I honestly don't need to wave a magic wand. I love my life! I have a great team, and we have amazing fun. I am happy and healthy, and my husband and I have a lot of fun together. That is ideal for us. We have gone to a ranch in the Tetons for the past 20 years. I don't need to travel elsewhere. I love to spend time with family and friends. Plus, I am grateful I have very fulfilling work that keeps me occupied.

Q: Have you ever worked with a financial advisor/planner before?

A: Yes, and I love her!

Q: What do you love best about working with them?

A: She is a good listener. She shares views, and I trust her. She helps with stock donations to charities.

Q: What else would you like from her that would make your experience even more valuable?

A: Nothing. We meet twice a year, and she is wonderful.

LET'S TALK ABOUT SOME CHALLENGES, FEARS, AND FRUSTRATIONS.

Q: What's the biggest thing holding you back or slowing you down from reaching your goal(s)?

A: I could and probably should reduce spending.

Q: What's your number one concern?

A: I don't really have a concern about financial security.

Q: What do you know now that you wish you would have known early on?

A: Reduce tax for your business. Find ways to reduce your taxes.

Kathy's Words of Wisdom: It's not worth your time to worry about money. It's an improper use of energy. Things were not always rosy for us. If we didn't have the money, we didn't spend. Some years, we lived frugally, and some years were good. Both my husband and I are self-employed and run our own businesses.

Connie's Insights: Her candid answers are helpful. She believes in tithing and putting money away for retirement and is rigid in those habits. She provides, perhaps, some thoughtful consideration of being frugal when necessary as she does not live outside of her means.

VALERIE THOMPSON

Current Position: Strategy Consultant;
Diversity, Equity & Inclusion

Q: What's most important to you about money?

A: Money provides security and comfortability. Knowing that your emergency fund and your "fun" money fund is full gives you security. My mom taught me to save. We were pretty risk averse growing up and usually in a state of lack. When I was growing up, I wanted to know that I was secure. I was taught that "It's easier for a camel to get through the eye of a needle than for a rich man to enter the kingdom of God," and that money is the root of all evil. Yet between going to church and interacting with others and learning more, I learned it's okay to make a lot of money. The Bible does not say, in fact, that money is the root of all evil, although it does warn that the love of money *can* lead to evil. I work with a financial coach right now, and he tells me to ask for more, seek out a higher paying job, and doors will open when you look for them.

Q: What do you really want that you don't have right now?

A: I have been self-employed since 2005. Currently, I would like to get to a point where I feel financially secure and create several streams of income for myself.

Q: What's your next big goal? What's the next level for you?
A: Multiple streams of income. I am working on 1) An online retail store that provides marketing materials to promote businesses. 2) Education: I am working to provide online classes. 3) My day job is in the design field.

Q: What do your finances look like in the future? Can you paint the picture for me?
A: Within a year, I want to be able to cover my living expenses with my entrepreneurial income. I have a passion for art and marketing. In ten years, I would like to travel and speak about increasing inclusion in the art and marketing industry.

Q: If you could wave a magic wand, what does life look like for you?
A: I would be traveling and speaking and helping organizations with diversity, equity, and inclusion.

Q: Have you ever worked with a financial advisor/planner before?
A: Yes. I've been working with a financial planner for the last six years.

Q: What do you love best about working with them?
A: He challenges me to think about things I haven't thought about before. My eyes kind of glaze over with these things, and he helps me to understand.

LET'S TALK ABOUT SOME CHALLENGES, FEARS, AND FRUSTRATIONS.

Q: What's the biggest thing holding you back or slowing you down from reaching your goal(s)?

A: I need passive income. Initial time and money to invest to get business started.

Q: What's your number one concern?

A: I'm tempted to live outside of my means. I'm good, but I must remind myself all the time that I need to sacrifice a little now to get where I am going.

Q: What do you know now that you wish you would have known early on?

A: Having an accountability source is important. Never be afraid to ask for help.

Valerie's Words of Wisdom: Be willing to be open to someone. It's not weakness.

Connie's Insights It's not easy for Valerie right now. She works hard and is striving to do even more. I love her spirit! She has a good mindset, but she could really benefit from working towards overcoming negative thoughts about money. I believe she will.

TEENA PICCIONE

Current Position: C-Suite Executive,
Global Transformation and Operations
Executive, Google

Q: What's most important to you about money?
A: We decided that my husband would stay at home with the children, and that I would be the sole provider for the family. That decision, put me in the position of carrying all the monetary burden for the family. Decisions are made differently because you don't have the freedom of two incomes. It brings an entirely different set of priorities: ensuring that there is money for college and retirement, and that as you look at life, you are making choices that are going to be the best for the family, not your career.

Q: What do you really want that you don't have right now?
A: I've learned to be content with whatever state I am at. I don't believe you must have all the toys. I believe you should have enough to be able to take care of yourself and family and then to share and give back. Giving to others is where true happiness comes from.

Q: What's your next big goal? What's the next level for you?
A: From a career perspective, I'd like to be a Chief Executive Officer or Chief Operating Officer. I enjoy it more than anything. Part of it

is being able to encourage, inspire, and excite people, and to knock it out of the park for the company that I'm working for.

Q: What do your finances look like in the future?

A: I want to make sure I have enough money to do what I want to do and have the freedom to. I have a home and a car. I've traveled to all fifty states, so that is done. We have two college kids about to graduate, and we adopted a child at age 17, and he's in the military right now. Cash flow will be freed up soon.

Q: If you could wave a magic wand, what does life look like for you?

A: I'd love to go back and travel to Canada and Ireland. I don't think I'd live differently if I were to win the lottery. We have our needs taken care of and most of our wants too. We figure out how to do it without going into debt. I want to give back. That means a lot to me!

Q: Have you ever worked with a financial advisor/planner before?

A: Yes, we always have. I believe we are not an expert on everything. We must utilize experts we have on our journey.

Q: What do you love best about working with them?

A: Ensuring that together we come up with a plan and we work the plan—even when the market is tanking. It should be so bulletproof that you continue any way you can.

LET'S TALK ABOUT SOME CHALLENGES, FEARS, AND FRUSTRATIONS.

Q: What's the biggest thing holding you back or slowing you down from reaching your goal(s)?
A: As far as career and becoming a CEO or COO when the opportunity comes, I will be ready.

Q: What's your number one concern?
A: I've planned for every contingency and gone deep for what that looks like. Nothing should hold us back.

Q: Is there anything that worries you?
A: No, I don't have time for that. I always laugh and say, 'Give it to God. He's up all night anyway.' It's not what keeps me up at night; it's what gets me up in the morning. Gods got it all night. Then I can look at the problem with fresh eyes in the morning.

Q: What do you know now that you wish you would have known early on?
A: Always say yes more than no, and know your line early on. Know what you're willing to do and what you're not willing to do. Draw the line in the sand and don't cross over.

Teena's Words of Wisdom: You have 86,400 seconds every day, use them well. Give back. Don't go into massive debt. I was first-generation high school and first-generation college. I got up at 3 a.m. to work at UPS. I worked during the day, and at night I went to school.

Connie's Insights: Teena's career meets the needs of her family. She is driven and diligent, and she approaches life with meticulous thoughtfulness. I love it!

GRACE LEVIN

Age: 46

Current Position: VP Director of Marketing for her own company.

Grace started her own business in 2015 while still working at a corporation. She is a digital-first marketer with a passion for and expertise in digital transformation, omni-channel marketing, product launches and full funnel marketing campaigns that drive meaningful business growth.

Q: What's most important to you about money?
A: My husband and I have always done well. Not long ago we were at perhaps the top of our earning career. It's a little different now. Our income is lower right now because I left my work at a big-name company last year in hopes of taking my own business to the next level. Sometimes that doesn't always work out the best for the family.

Q: What do you really want that you don't have right now?
A: Making sure I manage money appropriately to have financial flexibility would be wonderful. Salary *does* matter because living in LA is quite expensive. I would like to have the flexibility to take on any job I want that would provide the steady income we were used to.

Q: What's your next big goal? What's the next level for you?
A: To land my next big job. I put my own business on the back burner now for a minute so I can provide better for the family. We'd like to put our children through college with as little debt to them as possible.

Q: What do your finances look like in the future? Can you paint the picture for me?
A: In one year, probably pretty much the same as it is now, if not a little worse. I may have an opportunity to work at a startup, and in that case, it will obviously take a little time to help get off the ground. Ten years from now, I'd like to be winding it down from a corporate perspective and probably not in California.

Q: If you could wave a magic wand, what does life look like for you?
A: We would have no mortgage. Our children's college would be paid for, and I'd have a great job and good health insurance.

Q: Have you ever worked with a financial advisor/planner before?
A: Yes, we do.

Q: What do you like best about working with them?
A: He's approachable and proactive, and he understands the nuances of my husband's business. He's prone to diversify and sets up introductions for us like estate planning or anything else we may need.

Q: What else would you like from them that would make your experience even more valuable?

A: Maybe he could push us a little more but honestly, he has a good rapport with my husband, and we like that.

LET'S TALK ABOUT SOME CHALLENGES, FEARS, AND FRUSTRATIONS.

Q: What is the biggest thing holding you back or slowing you down from reaching your goal(s)?

A: I would have to say it is me *not* earning enough right now because the cost of living is ridiculous here in California. That can slow anyone down.

Grace's words of wisdom: When pursuing employment, choose good compensation even if you must negotiate it, and work for a company that has stock options that will be worth something someday.

Connie's Insights: Grace revealed that when things go wrong or not how we planned it, resiliency is necessary no matter our range of income. We will face difficulties from time to time. Many people would get down about it, but she is not. In fact, she is actively seeking ways to make things easier for her family. Bravo!

DEBY LEXOW

Current Position: Founder/Owner LOCLE Box

Deby knows that everyone loves to receive gifts. She is an Ohioan, and gifting from Ohio purveyors is her passion. She truly enjoys curating special gift boxes full of the freshest Ohio artisanal provisions and creative gift items.

Q: What's most important to you about money?
A: The most important thing to me about money is that I have enough to live comfortably for the rest of my life and to maintain the lifestyle I have grown accustomed to. As I was growing up, we never talked about money, and we never wanted for anything. I didn't know anything about money or even a checkbook or a savings.

Q: What do you really want that you don't have right now?
A: I love my life. I don't want for anything. I have money and health and education. I love learning and will continue to learn new things all the time.

Q: What's your next big goal? What's the next level for you?
A: To grow my business.

Q: What would be the most ideal situation for you right now? If you could wave a magic wand, what does life look like for you?
A: I would work less.

Q: Have you ever worked with a financial advisor/planner before?
A: Yes. I also have a CPA and an estate planning attorney.

Q: What do you love best about working with them?
A: I love that my financial advisor connected with my husband. That was huge for me because he was a little apprehensive about talking to anyone about our finances. I like regular communication with her—that personal contact. To pick up the phone and have a 10-minute conversation is very meaningful.

LET'S TALK ABOUT SOME CHALLENGES, FEARS, AND FRUSTRATIONS.

Q: What is the biggest thing holding you back or slowing you down from reaching your goal(s)?
A: Frustration in not knowing what's ahead in the market and even in life and how to improve my business.

Q: What's your number one concern?
A: Needing long term care. I don't want my children to have to take care of me, so we have talked about long term care insurance and if that is appropriate for me.

Q: What do you know now that you wish you would have known early on?
A: I wish I would have started my business and learned about good money strategies long ago.

Deby's Words of Wisdom: Take control now, whether you are in a relationship or single. Take control of your money and be responsible for it and for your future. Plan for the unexpected. You just don't know what life may bring, and you don't want to be caught without the means to get through whatever that may be.

Connie's Insights: Deby's focus is helping others. Through her business she provides a unique approach to gift-giving, which is basically an extension of her heart. I love her business approach in that all her gifts are from local artisans. So, in offering their specialties to her customers, she is promoting their businesses and products as well. She's all about lifting others by promoting them and encouraging small businesses to grow.

RACHEL ABBOTT

Age: 50

Current Position: CEO, a health, and services organization; Speaker, Author

Q. What's most important to you about money?

A: You need to be in control of your money. I had a husband who was just terrible with money, and our marriage imploded because of it. Now I have the control, and that is critical. I relied on him to take care of the money, and when I found out he wasn't doing that, it was too late. I felt like the rug was pulled out from under me. I won't let that happen again.

Q: What do you really want that you don't have right now?

A: I would like more confidence in my ability to retire. I have one child in college, and one almost done. Then I will have more to contribute to my own financial future.

Q: What's your next big goal? What's the next level for you?

A: I am going to Italy soon. That will be fun. I am taking care of my college children. I am focusing on what I can do now today to have a comfy retirement.

Q: What do your finances look like in the future? Can you paint the picture for me?

A: I am in a good spot. I live on a budget. In one year, I hope to have a substantial amount in my savings. In ten years, I am hoping that I will have accumulated a substantial amount for retirement.

Q: If you could wave a magic wand, what does life look like for you?

A: I'd like to make more money, but in the nonprofit world, that is a challenge. I am wired for charity work and for causes that I have interest in.

Q: Have you ever worked with a financial advisor/planner before?

A: No, but I am on a corporate board for a financial services company. So, I have a little exposure to financial planning.

Q: What do you think you would love best about working with them?

A: The holistic approach they take. I think they can help me leverage what I have so I can take care of myself and then others.

Q: What else would you like from them that would make your experience even more valuable?

A: I am not a high roller, but I would like my financial planner to make me feel like I am. If I knew I could get a good return by using a financial advisor, I would hire one hands down. It would be a game changer for me if I could get second opinions and get some recommendations. I am open to others' opinions.

LET'S TALK ABOUT SOME CHALLENGES, FEARS, AND FRUSTRATIONS.

Q: What's the biggest thing holding you back or slowing you down from reaching your goal(s)?

A: Since I lost so much in that situation with my ex-husband, I feel I have been behind the eight ball. It caused a set-back and it slowed me down.

Q: What one challenge would you love to be solved right now?

A: I feel like I am starting from scratch. I am on my own, with two college kids.

Q: What do you know now that you wish you would have known early on?

A: I wish I would have learned about money and understood it on my own and not have relied on my husband. Obviously, I think it's important now to be active in your own money matters. I didn't ask questions that I should have. Look at the math and make sure your own needs are met. You have a right to know.

Rachel's Words of Wisdom: Don't be intimidated by the language of financial people. They talk about mutual funds and Exchange Traded Funds (ETFs) and things that might seem complex. Just ask questions so that you understand. If I can do it, you can too.

Connie's Insights: This story is a blessing for our readers and offers a valuable lesson. Hopefully it will open people's eyes if they are in the same predicament as Rachel was. When it comes to money, it can be a costly mistake to allow someone else to have total control. The results can be devastating. I am a huge proponent of "know what your money is doing."

DR. CHRISTINE RICE

Age: 34

Current Position: Executive Healthcare
Operations Leader, Founder

Q: What's most important to you about money?
A: Money creates financial security and gives you stability. It's a tool for freedom. It can open doors for how you want to live.

Q: What do you really want that you don't have right now?
A: I have dedicated an enormous amount of time on education for many years, and that took a lot of money. I rent right now, but I would love to own a home of my own.

Q: What's your next big goal? What's the next level for you?
A: I am an Executive VP right now, but I want higher success by working on my own start up. I want to inspire transformational change for women and the underserved by creating a platform to make it easier for the minority to get good health care.

Q: What do your finances look like in the future? Can you paint the picture for me?

A: In one year, I see myself owning property. I think it's good to own real estate and believe it's a smart way to amass wealth. In ten years, I will have substantial savings—I am hoping in the millions— to invest and carry out my goals.

Q: If you could wave a magic wand, what does life look like for you?

A: I would be working for myself. My business would be launched already. And I would be in my new home! I'm not dating yet, but I would be married and have children. I am a millennial though, and I have that "job first" mentality.

Q: Have you ever worked with a financial advisor/planner before?

A: Yes. I have debt and student loans, but eventually I will be saving more in a Roth and saving for a new home.

Q: What do you love best about working with them?

A: They are transparent with me, and they educate me about investments and financial planning.

LET'S TALK ABOUT SOME CHALLENGES, FEARS, AND FRUSTRATIONS.

Q: What's the biggest thing holding you back or slowing you down from reaching your goal(s)?

A: Mental procrastination. I am coming from a place of so much study and schoolwork that I honestly just need a mental break right now.

Q: What's your number one concern?

A: That in ten years I am still where I currently am. I want to be much further along. I have a fear that I may not be where I want to be.

Q: What do you know now that you wish you would have known early on?

A: Living within your means is very important. It's okay to save. Establish credit, but do not rely on credit cards for anything.

Dr. Rice's Words of Wisdom: Women, take responsibility! Believe in yourself. Believe that you can do it and do it! You might surprise yourself and be better than men.

Connie's Insights: Interviewing a young woman who is so performance-driven is inspiring! Dr. Rice knows just what she wants and has worked very hard to get there! There is no doubt that her fear of staying where she is today is just that—a fear. (False Evidence Appearing Real).

NOW, LET'S MOVE ON TO ONE of my favorite and most flexible financial tools: Life Insurance. By the end of the next chapter, you'll understand why it's one of my favorites.

CHAPTER 5

Beyond Protection: Leveraging Life Insurance for Financial Freedom

You don't buy life insurance because
you are going to die . . . but because
those you love are going to live.

—Anonymous

LET'S TALK ABOUT A TOPIC we don't normally like to discuss, but I assure you, it's profoundly important. I believe life insurance serves as the bedrock of a strong financial plan. By securing this cornerstone of protection, your beneficiaries can avoid the need to liquidate hard-earned assets, ensuring they receive financial support without having to use up your assets and legacy. Stick with me here . . .

Did you know while more than half of Americans have life insurance, only half of them are adequately insured?[11]

Think about it for a minute. That means only half of the half that are insured have enough insurance. Essentially, that means three-quarters of American families will struggle after the death of the insured because there's not enough money to settle all debts, funeral costs, and other expenses. Let's make sure this doesn't happen to you. This problem is easy to solve, and most of the time, it's inexpensive.

What's the single *easiest* thing you can do that will positively impact your family in a profound and powerful way? Make sure you have adequate life insurance. Why is that important? Someone once told me: "It is a total blessing to know we have life insurance for my husband, but it took almost dying for him to finally look at life insurance for himself." That near fatality transformed that man's life forever. Tell me, does a child, spouse, or loved one depend on your income? What would happen to your family if you could no longer provide?

Yes, this sounds scary, and many people are uncomfortable talking about this subject. I get it. But this scenario is a potential reality and a worst-case scenario that needs to be prioritized and planned for. Losing a loved one is already such a traumatizing and stressful event that having to go through even more by experiencing severe financial difficulties seems unnecessary, especially when it can be avoided.

LET'S BEGIN WITH THE WHAT, WHY, AND HOW OF LIFE INSURANCE.

What is term life insurance?

Term life insurance covers your life for a certain "term." It is typically provided in 10-, 15-, 20-, or 30-year increments, depending on your age.

You pay a premium every month, and the insurance company promises to pay your family a lump sum of money upon your death.

Why do you need it?

When you have life insurance, your family doesn't have to worry about finances. And there's even more to the picture. Life insurance not only gives your beneficiaries money when they need it the most, but it also is usually a tax-free payment to them upon your death.

Life insurance can:

- cover burial expenses.
- pay for the mortgage, car, utilities, and even kids' school needs.
- help sustain your family's current standard of living.
- replace the income of the person who passed away if they were the breadwinner, or it can cover the costs of daycare if they were the primary caregiver.
- pay off debt.
- invest and provide long-term income if wanted/needed.

Once you determine that you need life insurance, you first need to apply for it. The process is easy, and a financial advisor or life insurance agent can assist.

Steps to Apply for Life Insurance

1. Decide how much you need to pay off debts and replace your income.
2. Complete an application (generally takes 5–10 minutes).
3. A professional financial advisor or life insurance agent enters your application information into an underwriting software system. You could be approved immediately, or you might need a mini-medical exam (just a quick blood and urine test).
4. If approved, I look at the options that will align with your goals. You don't have to decide the amount and duration on your own.
5. Pay the agreed-upon premium amount once you are approved.
6. Your policy is activated, and you are covered.
   It's that fast and easy. You can be approved within a day, or it may take a few weeks. If you buy it when you are young and healthy, your premiums are usually less and therefore more affordable! You can still buy it in your 30s, 40s, 50s, and even in your 60s—and *yes*, it's still worth it.

Why don't some people buy life absurance?

With the significant advantages of life insurance, you might wonder why some people don't bother to buy it. The most common responses are:

1. I think life insurance is too expensive.
2. I don't need it because I have plenty of assets that would cover my heirs or beneficiary(s).
3. I'll get to it eventually. I have too many things to worry about right now.
4. I have it through my employer. (This s fine, but you typically can't take it with you if you leave that employer.)

Let's also talk about an alternative to term life insurance: permanent life insurance.

What is permanent life insurance?

Permanent life insurance refers to coverage that *never expires as long as premiums are paid* and combines a death benefit with a savings (cash) component.

There are two types of permanent life insurance:
1. Whole Life: grows cash at a fixed rate.
2. Universal Life: usually grows cash at a higher rate than fixed whole life.

Both provide a death benefit, and both offer favorable tax treatment as well. Let me explain:

The growth of the savings component piece is generally tax-deferred, meaning the policyholder pays no taxes on any earnings if the policy remains active. It grows tax-free, which is a substantial benefit.

Permanent life insurance offers a tax-free death benefit, and a portion of your monthly premium goes into the cash-value account that accumulates on a tax-deferred basis. The policy owner may access the cash value, if needed, without triggering taxes. In short, it is a cash-accumulating vehicle you can use for various goals and reasons.

Ways to use the cash component might be as a supplement to retirement income, vacation funds for the future, and even real estate purchases. Permanent insurance is so flexible, and this is why I like to use it as a wealth builder. Remember some of the stories from Chapter 1?

Think about it this way: money in tax-deferred retirement accounts, such as your pension or 401k, SIMPLE or SEP, will eventually be taxed as ordinary income, so taxpayers with well-funded retirement accounts should bear this in mind and consider diversifying their money into an alternative investment vehicle, like permanent life insurance.

Three ways you can use permanent life insurance to help fund retirement and/or estate planning strategies:

1. Supplemental Retirement Income. What if you could have cash available to supplement your income in retirement that is tax-free?

If you have a "tax-free" permanent life insurance policy that you can take cash or income from, you effectively diversify your income because now you have a taxed bucket and a no-taxed bucket.

Example: At retirement, you can take part of your 401k or pension fund as income each year and part from your permanent life insurance policy as income each year. The 401k will be taxed as income, and the part from your life insurance will not be taxed.

It's a smart move if you can do it. And many people don't know about it or how to use it when they plan for retirement. That's where a knowledgeable financial planner comes in.

I am passionate about educating people about this wealth building tool and getting the word out. I love it because it offers powerful flexibility and numerous options.

2. Help Pay for Long-Term Care. Many retirees worry that their savings could be depleted later in life because of the escalating costs of long-term care. A long-term care rider attached to a life insurance policy could help pay for these expenses if needed.

Optional benefit riders are available for an additional cost and are subject to the contractual terms, conditions, and limitations outlined in the policy; however, they may not benefit all individuals. That's why working with a qualified financial planner can help determine what riders are appropriate for you.

Budgeting for Long-Term Care can help, of course.

At the time I was writing this book, Medicare was paying for up to 100 days in a skilled nursing facility after a qualifying hospital stay of three or more days and providing limited coverage for home health care. Medicaid pays for some long-term care services, but eligibility is based on the person's income and assets and often requires "spending down" to qualify.

Another option is called a **Hybrid Long-Term Care** policy, which provides a death benefit whether or not you use the Long-Term Care insurance it provides.

The older Long-Term Care policies used to work like this: You paid your premiums, but if you *never* needed Long-Term Care, you basically wasted your money. You paid into it for nothing. This **Hybrid policy**, in my opinion, is usually a better use of your money because at least you get a death benefit in exchange for the premiums you paid into it.

3. Leave a Tax-Free Legacy

Most sons and daughters who inherit IRAs must now empty the inherited IRA account within ten years, and heirs who are forced to take distributions (money) in their peak earning years could face large income tax bills.

On the other hand, if parents had left a permanent life insurance policy instead—or in addition to their other assets—the death benefit could provide a *tax-free inheritance*. So, implementing a life insurance policy to pass down to your heirs can be a *huge blessing and a wise alternative.*

Before implementing a strategy involving life insurance, you should make sure you are insurable. The cost and availability of life insurance depend on factors such as age, health, and the type and amount of insurance you are purchasing.

Life insurance can also act as a gift.

LET ME TELL YOU A STORY.

A young grandmother came in to ask what gift options might be available for her grandson's second birthday. She had money she wanted to contribute each month if we could provide a vehicle that could benefit him. We came up with a powerful plan using Indexed Universal Life Insurance that will cost her about $75 a month for a $250,000 death benefit *and* create cash value inside the policy. The cash value can become quite significant!

Since he is now two, there is *no* underwriting for him. That *alone* is meaningful because if he develops a serious illness as he gets older, he will not *need* to qualify for life insurance at a more expensive rate. He already has it.

As you may or may not know, once you develop a serious illness, your life insurance cost will most likely increase. So not only does the grandson's premium remain the same throughout his life, but she is also creating cash value inside the policy that gives him options to withdraw money for future events, such as college, a wedding, or a new house. Taking money out of the policy can be done tax-free, and there are no limitations on what he could use the money for.

The grandmother can let the grandson take over ownership of the policy when he gets older and has a job, or she can continue to pay the premiums herself. I love this idea and flexibility.

Now, you can understand why I say life insurance is the bedrock and cornerstone of a solid financial plan. It's a powerful vehicle that can provide great flexibility in establishing a sound future for you *and* your loved ones.

Note: In addition to the life insurance premiums, other costs include mortality and expense charges. If a policy is surrendered prematurely, there may be surrender charges and income tax implications. Any guarantees are contingent on the financial strength and claims-paying ability of the issuing insurance company. Again, working with a knowledgeable and qualified financial advisor or insurance agent can help you figure that out. There are going to be costs, but the benefits will far outweigh them, in my opinion.

IN THIS FIFTH SET OF INTERVIEWS, we bring together more profound insights and takeaways. These stories encapsulate the essence of financial empowerment, leaving you with a wealth of knowledge and inspiration to apply to your own life. One of the stories shares how taking a Leap of Faith put her exactly where she feels she is supposed to be.

Following these eight interviews, we'll explore another one of my favorite tools: annuities.

PERSONAL MONEY STORIES PART 5

ALYSSA QUINLAN

Current Position: CEO, Hindman Auctions

Alyssa is an experienced Business Development Officer with a history in fine art and finance.

She works with buyers and sellers of art all around the globe. She has been featured in *The Wall Street Journal* and was recognized as Women in the Workplace Forum in New York City.

Q: What's most important to you about money?
A: Security. Because without money, you are stressed and are not prepared for unknown circumstances. Money and savings create security.

Q: Is there anything you really want that you don't have right now?
A: A more comprehensive financial plan would be beneficial as we look ahead to the future. With recent news that by 2034, retirees may only receive part of their benefits, I want to ensure we have adequate savings for any unknown expenses or emergencies as well as for retirement and long-term health care.

Q: What's a big goal for you? What's the next level?
A: Personally speaking, I hope to be able to continue charitable giving in a more material way for many of the organizations I am passionate about. Professionally, I would like to grow the company and expand the firm's footprint internationally.

Q: What would you like your finances to look like one year from now and ten years from now?
A: In one year, I expect to have more robust savings and investment accounts and to have paid off any credit debt. A new house would be ideal as well. In ten years, I anticipate the kids going off to college and more peace of mind around our finances. Giving back to the community has always been important to us as well.

Q: What would be the most ideal situation for you right now? If you could wave a magic wand, what does life look like for you?
A: My husband just got a job that he loves, so that is wonderful. On the business side, my business has a balance sheet that is expanding our footprint in my field.

Q: Have you ever worked with a financial advisor before?
A: Yes, though not currently. When I worked at JP Morgan, we were assigned a private banker, but given that my husband and I both worked in finance, we have been managing our own accounts.

Q: What do you like best about working with an expert in the financial services field?

A: I like that financial advisors can look at things objectively and make overall recommendations based on their experience and expertise. We need a financial advisor who understands our needs and can help us best prepare for the future. Things are not always rosy. They need to understand our position and make appropriate recommendations guiding us toward our goals.

LET'S TALK ABOUT SOME CHALLENGES, FEARS, AND FRUSTRATIONS.

Q: What's the biggest thing holding you back or slowing you down from reaching your big goal(s)?

A: Sometimes, life has a way of getting you sidetracked. We like to travel and visit friends now and then. Spending money without a real budget is likely slowing us down from reaching certain goals.

Q: What do you know now that you wished you would have known early on?

A: Right out of college, a colleague essentially bragged about the amount of credit card debt she had and said everyone she knew had five figures of debt not including college debt. Instead of putting money aside in my early twenties when I didn't have many expenses, I bought clothes or things I didn't need. I wish I would have had more guidance and discipline to have started saving and investing earlier. Even when your earnings increase, you still need financial guidance.

Alyssa's Words of Wisdom: Trust in yourself, and don't be afraid of what you could do. I had goals and drive, and I received support throughout my life to accomplish my goals. You can too. Have the dream and take chances. Surround yourself with people who encourage you!

Connie's Insights: I love Alyssa's confidence in her abilities with money. I admire her wisdom to be prepared for unforeseen circumstances and that a financial advisor can help with that.

SHANDRA

Age: 41

Current Position: Principal of a legal services firm; family, juvenile and criminal litigator

Q: What's most important to you about money?
A: Money provides comfort and security. I don't seek excess though. The only luxury I want is the ability to travel.

Q: What do you really want that you don't have right now?
A: To be debt free. I have student loans and credit debt. A professional degree sets you back, especially as a public servant when you work in the government and public service arena. I worked sixteen years practicing law as a prosecutor and public servant, so I didn't have the income that an attorney in a larger firm would have.

Q: What's your next big goal? What's the next level for you?
A: I just started my own practice about four months ago. My next big goal is to make it a successful business.

Q: What do your finances look like in the future? Can you paint the picture for me?

A: In one year, I hope to have significant revenue from my practice. My husband has some health issues, and I want him to be able to retire and try something new. In ten years, we will have increasing savings and investments.

Q: If you could wave a magic wand, what does life look like for you?

A: I would have three things: 1) a house fund 2) a travel fund 3) an investment and retirement fund.

Q: Have you ever worked with a financial advisor/planner before?

A: No.

Q: What do you think you would like best about working with one?

A: I think they could help my family with money—what investments to choose and be able to create an account for my son. Growing up, my mom had a scarcity mindset and lived below the poverty level. As I grew up, she was still working her way to obtaining a comfortable income. We never really had excess money growing up, let alone money to save or invest. So that taught me scarcity. I am coming out of that mindset now.

LET'S TALK ABOUT SOME CHALLENGES, FEARS, AND FRUSTRATIONS.

Q: What's the biggest thing holding you back or slowing you down from reaching your goal(s)?
A: Too much credit card debt. It's like a heavy black cloud hanging over my head.

Q: What do you know now that you wish you would have known early on?
A: Well, I now know, because you, Connie, just shared with me that a SEP or a SIMPLE plan can help when you are self-employed by creating tax advantages in providing a retirement account for myself.

Shandra's Words of Wisdom: Kill the credit cards. I got one in college, and it became a crutch in law school. I became an attorney shortly before the recession of 2008, so I took the first job I was offered after law school, and it paid $36,000 as an attorney. I used credit cards to get by because $36,000 was not much of an income. My income covered student loans, rent, and food. Any extras had to be put on the card. So, I *strongly* say, "Don't use credit!"

Connie's Insights: Shandra shows us that no matter our status in life, we sometimes feel as if we are forced to make some short-term decisions without thinking about the long-term consequences. She knows what she needs to do now and will focus on it and take the necessary action steps to accomplish her goals. She also knows that a financial advisor can add so much value to her future.

PHOEBE JUJA

Age: 61

Current Position: Inventor

Phoebe has always been a problem solver; looking at common everyday challenges from a different perspective. After seventeen years of working for a corporation, she found herself unemployed in 2007. She saw it as an opportunity to follow her dream to become an entrepreneur. It was a simple vision. She created a product-driven company.

Q: What's most important to you about money?
A: Money means different things at different ages. Right now, I believe I have enough money to retire, but I have children ages 31, 28, and 24. My 28-year-old is engaged to be married next year. That makes you think about the cost of weddings and the effect it can have on my retirement savings.

Q: What do you really want that you don't have right now?
A: I handle my own 401k and investments. People talk about financial planning, and I guess I would like to know if I have enough to retire and if my investments will run out. I feel like thirty years ago I should have looked at that.

Q: What's your next big goal? What's the next level for you?
A: I am still working, and I enjoy launching products. So, I will keep doing what I do, but in between that, my goal is to live in a different place every year—to take "adventures" in different places.

Q: What do your finances look like in the future? Can you paint the picture for me?
A: The previous year proved to be exceptionally challenging. The impact of COVID-19 significantly disrupted my business operations, resulting in increased debts across the line of credit. Improving the income generated by my products and boosting revenues has become my primary focus. Looking ahead to the future, my aspirations involve achieving a debt-free status and establishing a well-structured succession plan for the business.

Q: If you could wave a magic wand, what does life look like for you?
A: My life would be very similar to what it is now, but without the worries.

Q: Have you ever worked with a financial advisor/planner before?
A: No. I don't feel I have enough money for it to be worth it. Also, I don't understand the cost of it. Usually, I hear they charge a 1% fee, so I ask myself, is it worth it? (Connie's Advice: Think about this: If you gain even a modest 8% on your investment and pay 1% for example, is that worth it? I think so. You gained a net of 7% that you may not have gained on your own).

Q: What do you think you would like best about working with them?
A: Having an additional perspective to review matters would be incredibly beneficial. However, I'd need to recognize the value it brings before making any commitments. While I previously didn't mind the fluctuations in the markets, the current scenario has changed for me. As retirement approaches, I've become less tolerant of market downturns and their effects.

LET'S TALK ABOUT SOME CHALLENGES, FEARS, AND FRUSTRATIONS.

Q: What is the biggest thing holding you back or slowing you down from reaching your goal(s)?
A: The macroeconomics are holding me back. They are out of my control.

Q: What's your number one concern?
A: Getting my lines of credit paid down. In over ten years, I have not encountered this issue before. Frankly, I don't like it.

Q: What do you know now that you wish you would have known early on?
A: Explore things. Don't make assumptions. Do the research.

Phoebe's Words of Wisdom: If everyone was perfect at managing money, we would all be wealthy. Your money is yours. It's your responsibility to manage it.

Connie's Insights: Regarding money and financial planning, Phoebe is apprehensive about paying someone for advice and to help her implement strategies for investing. I hope this book helps her.

184

SHERRY MARTIN, MBA

Age: 60

Current Position: Founder,
Corporate Training, Leadership Development,
Public Speaking, Team Building, Training,
HR Consulting

Q: What's most important to you about money?
A: That it provides savings for my retirement. I'm almost at retirement age.

Q: What do you really want that you don't have right now?
A: My ultimate goal is to have enough money to live comfortably and to travel. We are not extravagant people but like to enjoy experiences and friends without having to worry about money.

Q: What's your next big goal? What's the next level for you?
A: I would like to double what I made this year in my business next year.

Q: What do your finances look like in the future? Can you paint the picture for me?

A: In a year from now, if I can double my income, I will be able to sock a lot away into my retirement account. If I do that each year, by the time I retire, I should be at my goal.

Q. If you could wave a magic wand, what does life look like for you?

A: I would love to retire at 65. I would love to have the choice to continue to work or not. It makes it nicer when you have a choice and don't "need" to continue to work.

Q: Have you ever worked with a financial advisor/planner before?

A: Yes. I work with one right now. I plugged my own numbers in even before we met into an excel spread sheet. That gave us a starting point. I am an active participant. She honors that, and we work together to achieve the goal.

Q: What do you love best about working with them?

A: It gives me confidence. I know some things about investing, but I wanted to confirm that I am on the right track. I like that my advisor looks out for me. For instance, when the market recently tanked, she helped me get through it. I love that she is a fiduciary too! It makes me feel better.

Q: What else would you like from her that would make your experience even more valuable? A: Making sure that investment fees are the lowest while providing a possibility of the highest returns.

LET'S TALK ABOUT SOME CHALLENGES, FEARS, AND FRUSTRATIONS.

Q: What is the biggest thing holding you back or slowing you down from reaching your goal(s)?
A: The struggle to communicate to potential clients my worth and value. Creating a consistent client pool is the toughest thing.

Q: What's your number one concern?
A: The stock market, especially since I am five years away from retirement.

Q: What worries you about money?
A: That the money we have will not be enough. I saw my mom and grandma struggle. I don't want to be that person. My mom's planner should have told her she'd run out if she didn't slow down spending. My mom is in assisted living now. That can eat up savings and retirement funds rather quickly.

Q: What do you know now that you wish you would have known early on?
A: I should have saved more—and early on. I made a lot of money in my lifetime; I should have put more away for retirement. I started

way back when I was younger with a nice amount in my 401k. When times were tough, though, I borrowed from it, not realizing the effect that it would have. If I had just kept that growing, I would likely be in spectacular shape today. It would have grown exponentially in that 20 to 30-year period.

Sherry's Words of Wisdom: Do dollar cost averaging to create your retirement. In effect, it eliminates the effort required to attempt to time the market to buy at the best prices.

Connie's Insights: The most important thing to Sherry right now is her savings for retirement. Her go-getter attitude will take her far, and working with her advisor helps keep her on track to her goals.

REGINA DEBRO REMBERT

Age: 65

Current Position: Chief Executive Officer at Brightstar Consulting, LLC and Think Veterans First, promoting veteran owned businesses across the country.

Regina is a 22-year retired Army Veteran. She retired from the Military as the Chief Paralegal, 416th Theatre Engineer Command in 2010 with an Honorable Discharge.

Q: What's most important to you about money?
A: Money is necessary so you can take care of your family. My husband was forced to take a disability retirement because of a medical condition, so I have become the main breadwinner for the family. I have always worked more than one job to take care of the family, and I love what I do.

Q: What do you really want that you don't have right now?
A: I would like to build my company so that I can provide an income for us. In addition to providing HR training and consulting services, I published a book last year, *Think Veterans First: Pushing through the Pandemic for the Win.*

Q: What's your next big goal? What's the next level for you?
A: I started a nonprofit for veteran owned businesses in 2020 during the COVID-19. The purpose of the nonprofit is to bring awareness of our veteran owned businesses and what services they provide in our communities. I host an event each September called VET OHIO EXPO. I'd like to keep that growing.

Q: What do your finances look like in the future? Can you paint the picture for me?
A: My goal for this next year is to raise enough to pay the expenses and to contribute to the non- profit in a meaningful way. In ten years, I will be 75 sitting on a beach relaxing. I have retirement funds and a federal pension coming, but I have accumulated some debt from the nonprofit that I need to take care of before I fully retire.

Q: If you could wave a magic wand, what does life look like for you?
A: It would be great for someone else to be running the nonprofit so I can promote the book and work to strengthen Brightstar Consulting.

Q: Have you ever worked with a financial advisor/planner before?
A: Yes, since 2008.

Q: What do you love best about working with them?
A: I love that our financial affairs are in order. I am interested in long term care insurance, so I need to talk to someone about that. I am in good shape and expect to be line dancing at age 95.

LET'S TALK ABOUT SOME CHALLENGES, FEARS, AND FRUSTRATIONS.

Q: What's the biggest thing holding you back or slowing you down from reaching your goal(s)?

A: I just started the nonprofit, and I just started running Brightstar full-time this month. I have used a lot of my personal savings to start both businesses, so I am looking for a return on my investments. Getting the word out is the biggest thing holding me back right now.

Q: What's your number one concern?

A: Getting the proper funding for the nonprofit and keeping it afloat.

Q: What do you know now that you wish you would have known early on?

A: How important networks are and to keep those relationships alive. You never know when you may need them.

Regina's words of Wisdom: When you reach the top, be sure that you are looking back to pull someone else up.

Connie's Insights: Regina served in the military for over twenty years, and we thank her for that! In addition, I find her inspiring that at 65 she has started two new businesses. That is no easy feat!

ASHLEY POWELL

Age: 33

Current Position: Human Resources, Youth Ministry

Q: What's most important to you about money?
A: To have enough to pay my bills. To be able to feed my family and to be able to afford some things that we want. I would love to be able to give back to causes and organizations that are important to me too.

Q: What do you really want that you don't have right now?
A: I would like to be debt free. We purchased a house, and it's a money sucker. Property taxes, homeowners' insurance, and just fixing it costs a lot. I didn't intend for the weight of all that when I bought the house. I have two boys ages 16 and 4. They eat me out of house and home [she said with a smile]. Not stressing about buying clothes and food for them would be wonderful.

Q: What's your next big goal? What's the next level for you?
A: I grew up in poverty. Because of that, I want to be able to contribute to others not having to go through what I went through. I feel like there's a gap in our society. I am currently trying to find something that would provide passive income for us to be able to travel as well. I love to vacation.

Q: Have you ever had a financial planner?

A: No, but I have worked with United Way for budgeting and saving. They help review your spending and find ways to help you let go of spending on the things that are not so important.

Q: What do you think you would like best about working with a financial advisor?

A: I would like to work with someone who doesn't make me feel uncomfortable about talking about my money situation. I'd like someone who doesn't make me feel inadequate when I ask a question about money. I am embarrassed talking about finances because I feel like I should know better when I make decisions.

LET'S TALK ABOUT SOME CHALLENGES, FEARS, AND FRUSTRATIONS.

Q: What's the biggest thing holding you back or slowing you down from reaching your goals?

A: Me! I'm holding myself back because of my negative self-talk—telling myself things like, "Go ahead and spend. I can 'make up' for it on the next payday."

Q: What's your number one concern?

A: Ensuring that I do enough for my children and that I am providing well for them.

Q: What do you know now that you wish you would have known early on?
A: That I am strong and able to take the first step and start to save! If you have a fear of failure, don't listen to it! Blast past it.

Ashley's Words of Wisdom: You can do anything you put your mind to. And I know that sounds super cliché, but if you just take that first step and start, that's the hardest thing to do.

Connie's Insights: Ashley's experience with money and feelings toward finances are mixed, not only because of her current situation, but also because she was brought up in a household that was financially less equipped than others. She is working on a different mindset now! I love that!

LAURA SACHA

Age: 53

Current Position: Chief Operating Officer, Legatus International

Over twenty years ago, Laura took a leap of faith when she left the practice of law to spend more time with her young children. Not a month later, her Catholic diocese posted an ad for a part-time position with Legatus. Thus, began not only a career change, but also a faith journey that built her trust in God's provision and plan for her life.

Q: What's most important to you about money?
A: I don't like money, to be honest with you. It can be the cause of so much stress and tension. One way of mitigating this stress as an adult was to work within our family to position ourselves to be able to live on one income and to have a mindset of always living within our means. Savings has always been important to us as well. I think money is very useful for the purpose of providing for your needs and for giving back.

Q: What do you really want that you don't have right now?
A: We are kind of in between right now, meaning most of the kids have flown the coop, and we are looking to an early retirement for

my husband. Right now, I want to be able to forecast what our future living and leisure activities will look like; for example, a vacation home where all the children will be able to gather and create memories.

Q: What is your next big goal? What's the next level for you?
A: I am a new grandmother. This has sparked ideas for the future and leaving a legacy of some type for the children, regardless of how modest. The next level would be to pay off the mortgage, buy a new home, and have funds for the kids.

Q: What do your finances look like in the future? Can you paint the picture for me?
A: In one year, I think we will have more independence because the children will be on their own for the most part and living more independently, both emotionally and financially. In ten years, Doug, my husband, will be retired, and I will likely still work part time because I like my work. We plan to spoil the grandkids and enjoy life.

Q: If you could wave a magic wand, what does life look like for you?
A: I would love to buy a lake house. Doug would be able to retire and pursue his love of photography.

Q: Have you ever worked with a financial advisor/planner before?
A: No. We have an accountant who does our taxes. I would like to talk with a financial advisor though; I think it would be helpful to us. (Of course, I agree! -Connie).

LET'S TALK ABOUT SOME CHALLENGES, FEARS, AND FRUSTRATIONS.

Q: What's the biggest thing holding you back or slowing you down from reaching your goal(s)?
A: Creating time and really talking about a concrete plan with my husband. It would be ideal to have a financial plan and be able to see possibilities.

Q: What challenge would you love to be solved right now?
A: I would like to taste the experience of freedom with money, and with the kids growing and moving on, that becomes easier because it will free up our cash flow.

Q: What do you know now that you wish you would have known early on?
A: The quicker you pay off debt, the more freedom you provide for yourself. I would suggest putting all your eggs in paying off debt. Debt strangles you. Student loan debt strangles you.

Laura's Words of Wisdom: Decide for yourself what is negotiable and non-negotiable for the way you want to live. Build your life around that. My being with my kids as they grew up was non-negotiable; I didn't mind sacrificing to be with them. For others, education or a big house is non-negotiable. Whatever it is, write it down and build your life around it.

Connie's Insights: For Laura, it was most important to be home and available for the kids. She was able to do that because they sacrificed two incomes for one. I like her words of wisdom: "Know what is negotiable in your life and what is not. Build from there."

NEXT, WE TURN TO ONE OF MY MOST trusted financial planning tools that can provide certainty when you need it: annuities—a powerful instrument for securing long-term financial stability.

CHAPTER 6

Annuities: A Reliable Retirement Strategy

I may take risks in life, but I will never
risk my money. I use annuities, and I
never have to worry about my money.

— Babe Ruth

IMAGINE PAINTING EVERYTHING YOU WANT for your retirement on a big, blank canvas. Would you finally travel the world or stay local to watch your grandkids grow up? Would you buy a house with a lakeside view or start that business you've been talking about?

Unfortunately, many people have a gap between their income needs during retirement and what they will actually receive because

199

of their current investing strategy. Others have lost money during market downturns or have withdrawn money because they fear losing it when things go south. If you're looking for a steady, guaranteed income stream, you may want to consider an annuity.

WHAT IS AN ANNUITY?

An Annuity is a *customizable* contract with an insurance company that allows you to receive guaranteed, regular payments.

Many people like the idea of using guaranteed income annuities to give them a safe and secure retirement, with a 100% guarantee of not losing your principal.

The first lifetime income annuities date back 2000 years to the Roman Empire. Citizens and soldiers would deposit money into a pool, and those who lived the longest would get increasing income payments, and those who weren't so lucky passed on. The government would take a small cut, of course. You gave them your money, and they promised you a guaranteed income or return on your money. After making your contribution, you got to decide when to start receiving income payments. The longer you waited, the higher your income payments would be. You would be presented with a schedule that showed the exact payment, so there is no guessing.

Every annuity contains two phases: the accumulation phase and the distribution phase. You know—put money in, then take money out. **The *accumulation phase*** is the period when you put money through premiums into the annuity. Depending on the type of annuity, this money may grow with interest and/or can be invested into a fund that fits your risk tolerance and future objectives.

Now, remember when I said that annuities provide guaranteed income? In your contract, you decide when/if to start receiving (and the duration of) your income stream. For example, you may be able to receive your payments immediately or when you turn 65. You can set it up so that income may be paid for twenty years or until you or your spouse dies. You set it up with the help of your financial advisor in a way that will work best for you.

This process of receiving payments begins **the *distribution phase.*** This has helped many people cover life expenses in retirement, senior living care, or ensure they won't have to rely on their children to cover their future expenses.

Whatever your goals, an annuity can help your investment grow with interest and provide payouts when you need them most. But what happens if the market takes a downturn?

Fixed Annuities come with a minimum rate guarantee offered at the beginning of your contract. This allows you to take advantage of a portion of market increases while protecting your investments from market downturns.

As you near retirement, this may also give you an opportunity to transfer investments from more aggressive avenues to a safer route that accumulates growth while still paying out guaranteed distributions for as long as you decide. So, the question is will you need both a steady and guaranteed stream of income for retirement?

As an example, here's one way to use an annuity later in your retirement:

Imagine you want guaranteed income starting at age 80 or 85 until your passing. Knowing you have income secured at that stage allows you to plan for just 15 or 20 years of retirement initially. So, you save and invest enough to cover your expenses from age 65-80.

Then, you take another $100,000 and invest it in an annuity.

For instance, if a 65-year-old invests $100,000 in an Immediate Annuity, they could receive about $7,600 annually for life. However, if they instead put that $100,000 into a long-term deferred fixed income annuity that begins paying out at age 80, their annual income could be around $63,000.

The best part is this strategy allows you to save and invest for only 15 or 20 years rather than 30 or 35. If you live an additional 15 years beyond age 80, you could receive $63,000 per year, significantly more than your initial $100,000 investment. What do you think about that?

With the almost countless options available with annuities, you and a financial advisor can design a solution that works best for you and your family. The goal is to make sure your income is enough to cover expenses and that your annuity contract minimizes fees while maximizing payouts.

Questions to Ask Before You Buy an Annuity

- Is it a Fixed Annuity or another type, and what are the differences?
- Is there a chance I can lose my principal? (pertinent to Fixed or a Variable Annuity, but not pertinent to a Fixed Equity Indexed Annuity)
- What are the benefits of this specific Annuity?
- What are the disadvantages? Know them up front!
- Does this Annuity have any Guaranteed Benefits?
- Minimum guaranteed rate of return

- Guaranteed lifetime withdrawal benefit
- What are my payout options later when/if I "annuitize," meaning to start to take payments?
- Is there a death benefit?
- What are the fees associated with this Annuity?
- Are there any riders included, and what are the benefits of the riders?
- A Long-Term Care Rider
- Guaranteed Lifetime Income Rider
- What are the tax repercussions of my Annuity when I annuitize or take withdrawals?
- Is there a reduction of contract values when withdrawals are made?
- Are there surrender charges and penalties assessed, and are there reductions in the contract's values when a surrender is made during the surrender period?

I believe you've worked hard throughout your life, and it's worth it to finish strong and live the life you really want to live.

Quick story:

Meet Sarah, a retired schoolteacher who had diligently saved throughout her career but was concerned about outliving her savings in retirement. Upon retiring, at the recommendation of her financial advisor, Sarah decided to invest a portion of her savings into an annuity. The annuity provided her with guaranteed monthly payments in addition to her pension and social security for the rest of her life, ensuring she could maintain her standard of living in retirement.

With the steady income from her annuity, Sarah was able to enjoy retirement without worrying about market fluctuations or outliving her savings. She traveled the world, pursued her hobbies, and spent quality time with family and friends.

Even during times of economic uncertainty, Sarah's annuity continued to provide her with a dependable source of income, allowing her to weather financial storms with confidence.

That is one of the reasons I love the annuity. Your income doesn't have to change, and it is not dependent on how the market is doing.

If you want to find out if there is an annuity solution for you, talk to a financial advisor. You might be able to spend your retirement the way you want to! Or it may turn out better than you could have imagined.

Annuities are designed to be long-term investments and frequently involve charges such as administrative fees, annual contract fees, mortality, and risk expense charges, as well as surrender charges. Early withdrawals may impact annuity cash values and death benefits. Taxes are payable upon withdrawal of funds. An additional 10% IRS penalty may apply to withdrawals prior to age 59 1/2. Annuities are not guaranteed by FDIC or any governmental agency and are not deposits or other obligations of or guaranteed or endorsed by any bank or savings association. Guarantees are based on the claims paying ability of the issuing insurance company. Fixed Indexed Annuities are insurance products and not considered a security or investment.

THE FOLLOWING FINAL SET of interviews offers powerful wisdom, with each story inspiring action. One encourages, "Go for what you want." Another advises, "Create a plan." And a third reminds us, "Your life happens by the actions you take, not by intention." Their advice is both motivating and empowering, urging you to take charge and make things happen. Enjoy!

PERSONAL MONEY STORIES PART 6

GILLIAN SWENY

Age: 34

Current Position: Director of Marketing, Agileblue

Q: What's most important to you about money?
A: Money provides a comfortable lifestyle, providing us the things we need and the nicer things we don't necessarily need but we like to have.

Q: What do you really want that you don't have right now?
A: I have worked at a startup since 2021, and I get a base salary and bonuses. I will grow as the company grows.

Q: What's your next big goal? What's the next level for you?
A: A large savings account and to contribute more to my Roth and 401k. We started a 529 plan for our son who is two. My goal is to keep contributing and increase the contributions as we can.

Q: What would be the most ideal situation for you right now? If you could wave a magic wand, what does life look like for you?
A: We don't have a ton of debt, but I'd like to be debt free. I don't want to think about money and how much money is left at the end of the month.

Q: Have you ever worked with a financial advisor/planner before?
A: Yes. We have someone who has helped us with our 401k rollovers, and he set up an IRA that we invest in.

Q: What do you love best about working with them?
A: We wouldn't be where we are right now without him. We found him in our twenties, and he's helped a lot. I like at the end of each year he will have a conversation with us.

Q: What else would you like from them that would make your experience even more valuable?
A: I wish he would push us a little more—educate us on investing in the market.

LET'S TALK ABOUT SOME CHALLENGES, FEARS, AND FRUSTRATIONS.

Q: What's holding you back or slowing you down from reaching your goal(s)?
A: I am paid too little. My husband and I have separate monies. That's how we stay happy together. We each have our own and don't share funds.

Q: What's your number one concern?
A: I have an irrational fear that money will go away—that something will go wrong, and I will lose it all.

Q: What challenge would you love to be solved right now?
A: I would like my debt to be paid off. I am almost finished. The birth of our child took a lot of money, and I have about $600 left to pay from an $18,000 bill. I have a couple of credit cards to pay off as well, but only a couple thousand there.

Q: What do you know now that you wish you would have known early on?
A: I wish I knew more about saving and putting money aside. It's important to talk about money and to make plans and set goals. Face your fears about money. I never thought I would have the home that I have today. My dreams are coming true.

Connie's Insights: I like Gillian's spunk! She knows she should be making more and knows it will come in time. She is committed to her plans and goals. Her focus and discipline will get her to where she is going.

BEVAN EVANS

Age: 60

Current Position: Business Owner/President,
Evans Industries, Inc., Product Manufacturing

Since she was twenty, Bevan has been working with her mother as a
woman-owned business in manufacturing.

**Q: What's the most important thing to you about money
and creating financial freedom?**
A: Money means security to me. I am trying to grow my business to a
point where I can sell it and create a cash flow from it that will provide
a sustainable retirement income. My goal is to build the business and
sell it in seven years.

Q: What do you really want that you don't have right now?
A: Time to travel the world. I love England, and I want to travel
Europe and Asia. I would love to do a once-a-year trip to just get away.

Q: What do you want your wealth to look like in the future?
A: In one year, I will be continuing saving for retirement and build
our business. In five years,

I hope to buy a new building for the business. In ten to twenty years, I will have sold the business and retired, have the house paid off, and looking towards achieving the next ten-year-goal: 81- years-old and still alive, enjoying life, traveling the world.

Q: Have you ever worked with a financial advisor?
A: No. I have never used a financial advisor, and I only regret one thing: I could have started younger in planning and saving for retirement.

Q: What do you think you'd like best if you did decide to work with a financial advisor?
A: I think it would provide a clearer picture of retirement for me. I would rely on their expertise to fill in weak spots. Working with them would help take me from where I am to where I would like to be financially.

LET'S TALK ABOUT SOME CHALLENGES, FEARS, AND FRUSTRATIONS.

Q: What's the biggest thing holding you back or slowing you down from reaching your goal(s)?
A: The city, county, and state. As a woman-owned business, it's difficult to get through the bureaucracy that comes from the city, county, and the state. I also need to find a bigger building. That's not easy. I am just now finding out what I need to do to be eligible for some of the women- owned business incentives.

Q: What's your number one concern right now?

A: Getting additional product offerings so we can grow. The work that it requires to get the business to where I want is a major undertaking and feels like an uphill climb.

Q: Are there any opportunities where you feel like you may be leaving money on the table?

A: I don't know if I am truly optimizing the good things I have like my savings and investments.

Q: What do you know now that you wish you would have known early on?

A: It's not so much what I wish I knew; it's what I wish I could have done when I was younger—putting more money aside and planning for unforeseen things sooner.

Bevan's Words of Wisdom: Save early, save often.

Connie's Insights: Financial planning would help Bevan immensely to provide a clear picture of her future. Succession planning for business owners should begin at least 3-5 years prior to selling or passing it down to family. There are important things you need to have in place for a successful sale or even the transition to family.

CHRISTI K.

Age: 50

Current Position: President, CPA Firm Inc.

Q: What's most important to you about money?
A: Money to me means financial security. I don't want to have to worry about where the grocery money is coming from or how we will pay the bills. I never want to be so focused on money that I forget to enjoy life.

Q: What do you really want that you don't have right now?
A: More of a savings built up. That way I know I have financial security.

Q: What is your next big goal? What's the next level for you?
A: To buy a building that I can run my business from in Westlake or Avon, OH. I'd like it to be close to a highway so my clients can easily get to me. I am working with a realtor right now to make that a reality.

Q: What do your finances look like in the future? Can you paint the picture for me?
A: In one year, I would have my small debt paid off, so I can apply more money toward the new building. In ten years, I would like

to start winding down my career. I would do that by hiring more employees in the next few years and help them to grow so that they can eventually buy me out of the business.

Q: If you could wave a magic wand, what does life look like for you?

A: If I had a "pause" button, that would be ideal. [Laughing] Life comes at you so quickly, and I really need to remind myself to slow down. It's okay to take a minute here and there.

Q: Have you ever worked with a financial advisor/planner before?

A: No, but I would like to hire one.

Q: What do you think you would like best about working with them?

A: I would like to work with one so I feel a bit more control, and I think they can help me create a tax-free bucket for retirement. My husband is an attorney, and I love having an attorney in the family because he provides guidance too. I would like to start contributing to a retirement fund soon, and I know a financial advisor can help me with that.

LET'S TALK ABOUT SOME CHALLENGES, FEARS, AND FRUSTRATIONS.

Q: What's the biggest thing holding you back or slowing you down from reaching your goal(s)?
A: Probably to find the right building. I want it to be a professional building that I can maybe rent out and use as investment property.

Q: What challenge do you have you would love to be solved right now?
A: Time. I wish I had more of it. The kids take a lot from me. Time and money. Sometimes that is very overwhelming.

Q: What do you know now that you wish you would have known early on?
A: I took over this business from another accountant and felt like I had to say yes to every client because I needed the business from them. I was desperate for every little piece of work, but once you get things in place, you can be a little choosier. I wish I would have known that it is okay to say no to certain people, that I had more of a choice. You don't have to say yes to everyone. Be choosy as a business owner and work with those people you really like and are enjoyable to work for and with.

Christi's Words of Wisdom: You don't have to go it alone. Reach out to others for ideas and suggestions. Get opinions. Be open to advice. It will help you in the long run. Know your zone of genius as well. Know what you are good at and stick to doing that. Let people support you in your weaker areas.

Connie's Insights: Christi started the business on her own in 2010. She is now scaling it to make it work for her future. Working with a financial advisor could absolutely help her in her personal and business life. She could set up that tax-free bucket she talked about with their help as well as gain clarity for her financial future.

MIRANDA HILL

Age: 52

Current Position: VP of Finance, Controller, Sales & Marketing, Principal of an IT company

Q: What's most important to you about money?
A: Money provides the ability to do what I want when I want. I like to do a couple vacations each year. My kids are in private school, so money helps with tuition. Money provides safety and security and enables us to do what we enjoy. Giving back to the community is important to us as well, and money lets us do that.

Q: What do you really want that that you don't have right now?
A: I would like the ability to retire. My partner and I want to sell the business in a couple of years.

Q: What's your next big goal? What's the next level for you?
A: After I sell the business, I will volunteer for numerous things. I am very active with the children and their sports. I love to garden as well.

Q: What do your finances look like in the future? Can you paint the picture for me?

A: I could retire right now. I have enough money to do that without selling the business. However, my retirement could look even better if I hang in there and retire at age 60.

Q: If you could wave a magic wand, what does life look like for you?

A: I would have sold the business for a lot of money. I would get an RV and travel throughout the US. I'd have more lunches with my mom and spend time in New Jersey with some of my family. We would have 100% of what we currently make as income and continue to live the lives we are accustomed to but be able to enjoy going out more when we want to.

Q: Have you ever worked with a financial advisor/planner before?

A: Yes.

Q: What do you love best about working with them?

A: We've worked with one for over twenty years now. He did our 401k for our business, and we love the convenience of working with him on a personal level too. He does annual reviews for us and is forward thinking. We like that.

LET'S TALK ABOUT SOME CHALLENGES, FEARS, AND FRUSTRATIONS.

Q: What is the biggest thing holding you back or slowing you down from reaching your goal(s)?
A: The economy could be slowing us down if people are scared to spend money. Our business is dependent on how the economy is doing. We are changing things some to create consistency in revenue and moving to a subscription-based revenue stream.

Q: What do you know now that you wish you would have known early on?
A: In the first couple of years of the business, we didn't have a strategic plan. It's very important to make decisions and have action plans in place and carry them out.

Miranda's Words of Wisdom: Go for what you want. This was my first job out of college. My partner is a long-time friend. We were competitive athletes together. I'd say if you want it, find a way to make it happen. For the woman who wants it all, entrepreneurship is the answer!

Connie's Insights: I love Miranda's clear vision. She sees what she needs to do to increase revenues to make the business scalable and sell it in a few years. She has a plan. That's what gives her the confidence to move forward.

BARBARA DANIEL

Age: 79

Current Position:
Publisher/Editor;
The Cleveland Women's Journal

The Cleveland Women's Journal is designed to educate, energize, and empower women. The publication has been effective in promoting women and their entrepreneurial spirit.

Q: What's most important to you about money?
A: Having money in a safe place is important to me now, and I am conservative because of my age. I have an annuity that generates guaranteed income for me. The magazine is no longer in print, only digital. I hope to sell it and possibly retire in two or three years.

Q: What do you really want that you don't have right now?
A: I don't really want anything that I don't already have. The money is there when I need it.

Q: What do your finances look like in the future? Can you paint the picture for me?

A: I will be just fine because of financial planning. I have *always* worked, so I will volunteer somewhere. I love animals, so I see myself as a volunteer doing something with animals.

Q: Have you ever worked with a financial advisor/planner before?

A: Yes. I used to work for a securities company. I did estate and business planning, but I did not get involved with the investment side. I wasn't sure about which investments to invest in.

Q: What do you love best about working with them?

A: I love that they have a high degree of knowledge and integrity. They have knowledge I was lacking about which investment vehicles to choose and which would suit me best. I have a high level of trust in them. I like that we set up a whole life insurance plan for each grandchild. Whole life insurance pays dividends, and we use the dividends to pay the premiums for the grandkids.

LET'S TALK ABOUT SOME CHALLENGES, FEARS, AND FRUSTRATIONS.

Q: Are there any areas where you feel you might not be capitalizing on all the opportunities or leaving money on the table?

A: My husband and I had an estate plan when he died. We were prepared. Everything went to me and the children. We had a will and a trust, and I still do. I knew the importance of having those things in place. So, I don't think I am leaving money on the table anywhere. I feel good about what we had set up and what I still have in place now.

Barbara's Words of Wisdom: Stop thinking that you don't have enough. Focus on what you *do* have and be smart about how you use it. Stop and think, "Is this a good decision?" Have a savings account. Have an investment account. One should be a conservative fund (savings), and one can be a little more aggressive, depending on you and how aggressive you would like to be.

Connie's Insights: Barbara has truly given us some words of wisdom. Because of her age and experiences in life, I think it's admirable for her to look back and not have any regrets.

MELISSA FERRARO

Age: 48

Current Position: CEO, Nonprofit

Q: What's most important to you about money?
A: I think money provides stability and security. I have some anxiety around money for sure, but I try to create stability for the family. My mom and dad were high functioning alcoholics. My dad was an entrepreneur always looking for the next best thing. None of the things really panned out. His last job was being a cab driver. He always talked about a good work ethic. He wanted to leave a legacy for his family. That didn't happen. There was a legal battle for custody, and I found no support from my mom either.

Q: What do you really want that you don't have right now?
A: I would love student loan forgiveness as I am pursuing a doctorate. It's my biggest challenge.

Q: What's your next big goal? What's the next level for you?
A: I am the CEO for a nonprofit, and I love it. I consult and help companies with organizational development and human resources.

Q: What do your finances look like in the future? Can you paint the picture for me?

A: In one year, I will have my doctorate. I'm passionate about social justice and the nonprofit world. I see myself consulting and teaching and making an impact. My salary will be very good, but I don't do this work for the money. I do it for the impact.

Q: Have you ever worked with a financial advisor/planner before?

A: No. I am a first generation with a doctoral degree. I don't have a financial background, so I don't understand a lot when it comes to money and what my options are, so I would like some help with financial planning.

LET'S TALK ABOUT SOME CHALLENGES, FEARS, AND FRUSTRATIONS.

Q: What's the biggest thing holding you back or slowing you down from reaching your goals(s)?

A: Belief in myself. I am likely holding myself back. Isn't that true for many of us? We don't give ourselves the esteem that we should.

Q: What's your number one concern?

A: Self-care. I am a wife, a mom, a CEO, and a student. I am sure I don't sleep enough or eat like I should or take care of myself like I need to.

Q: What challenge would you love to be solved right now?
A: Student loan debt to be paid off would be a dream. Having a robust savings set aside would be another challenge right now.

Q: What do you know now that you wish you would have known early on?
A: I know now that I have a voice, I can ask for what I want, and I am *very worthy*! When you get a couple of negative words thrown at you all the time as you grow up, you start to believe them and think negatively about yourself. I never had people speaking positive words into my life for most of my young life.

Melissa's Words of Wisdom: Invest in yourself. If you want stability, create it. Make it happen. You can! If you want education, create it. Make it happen. You can! Your life happens by the action you take, not by intention!

Connie's Insights: Melissa had a tough life; her mom and dad obviously both had a disease. She has obviously come a long way from her beginnings. It's incredible that she is getting a doctoral degree to help others! Her determination is applaudable and makes me smile! She also understands that for her financial future she is not the expert, and she is open to working with someone to help make those dreams come true and create the stability and security she wants.

DR. MARIA CHASE, CM, LPCC, LICDC

Age: 60

Current Position: Family Counselor

Q: What's most important to you about money?
A: Security. Having enough money to be able to afford retirement costs like living expenses and medical care. I have savings, and I add to it regularly, but I am apprehensive about investing in the stock market because I have witnessed wealthy people lose money.

Q: What's your next big goal; what is the next level for you?
A: To get a better work-life balance. I work many, many late nights and early mornings.

Q: What does your financial wealth look like a year from now and ten years from now?
A: In one year, I would like to have more money saved to feel a little more secure. In ten years, I'd like to retire. I know I will have social security, and I'm hoping to have at least a decent amount in savings or an investment vehicle.

Q: If you could wave a magic wand what would life look like for you?
A: If I could wave a magic wand, I would love to have a house and maybe remarry.

Q: Do you work with a financial advisor?
A: No. I have already seen a financial advisor. When it is time, I will most likely talk to a senior citizen attorney for guidance.

Q: What's the biggest thing holding you back or slowing you down from reaching your big goals and buying that dream house?
A: I don't make a lot of money as a social worker.

Q: What challenge would you love to be solved right now?
A: I would like to retire at 70. My main worry is saving for retirement and having certainty about being able to receive and pay for medical care. I have high blood pressure and high cholesterol, and it worries me that at some point I might not have enough money to pay for my own medical care and insurance.

Q: What do you know now that you wish you would have known early on?
A: I wish I knew how expensive it is to own a home. My dad was very sick in his last years on earth, and I helped to take care of him. When he died, I sold the house to a real estate flipper, and I felt like I was backed into a corner without any options. It was not a good place to be and has probably scarred me in some ways.

Dr. Chase's Words of Wisdom: It's very important to utilize your resources and be open to opinions other than your own.

Connie's Insights: In Dr. Chase's work, she cares for people. Having an impact on others' lives is more important to her than having money.

ANNETTE GARSTECK

Age: 48

Current Position: Founder,
Garsteck Career Coaching: Empowering Women to
Reinvent Their Career, Rediscover Professional Purpose, and
Redefine Success; Former Fortune 50 Hiring Manager

Q: What's most important to you about money?
A: It provides experiences, and I wanted to prove to myself that it is possible to make a lot of money and that I can do it! The idea of money for me has evolved over time. As I grew up, we didn't have a lot of money. We didn't talk about money and the challenges you could have with it. Money provides for my future and helps me to provide for my family.

Q: What's your next big goal? What's the next level for you?
A: I am writing a book. I am all about career women. They need to be able to track their successes and realize the value they bring when they are changing careers. I have created a 1-to-1 coaching model and am bringing it into a group coaching model.

Q: What do your finances look like in the future? Can you paint the picture for me?

A: Right now, I take care of my mother-in-law, and then I anticipate I will be helping my mom as well. So not much of a change within the year. In ten to twelve years, I would like to retire to a warm and sunny place.

Q: If you could wave a magic wand, what does life look like for you?

A: I have a good life right now. I would love to have more time and space to fast track my business.

Q: Have you ever worked with a financial advisor/planner before?

A: Yes. When I rolled over my old 401k and pension.

Q: What do you like best about working with them?

A: Knowing that someone is watching the trends for me. I love that I don't have to be the expert, that someone will tell me if I need to know anything. I can see what's going on, and when the news is bad, I can look at it and still feel okay and that I'll get through.

Q: What else would you like from them that would make your experience even more valuable?

A: We meet quarterly and review accounts to reallocate every six months. There isn't really anything else I need.

LET'S TALK ABOUT SOME CHALLENGES, FEARS, AND FRUSTRATIONS.

Q: What challenge do you have that you would love to be solved right now?
A: I would like to have clearer milestones for myself. More clarity for my business.

Annette's Words of Wisdom: Use credit as a tool and not a long-term solution. When I was in school full-time, I packed on a lot of student loan debt. I stopped going full-time and went part- time to make it easier for myself.

Connie's Insights: I find it beautiful that she is okay with slowing down a little as life brings her an in-law to take care of—and eventually her mom. When things change, she can go back full force again if she chooses. Setting oneself up for important potential transitions such as this should be a consideration. Annette is wise to have done this, and it is ideal that she has the option and freedom to care for loved ones.

CHAPTER 7

My Thoughts on Money and True Wealth

*The secret to wealth is simple: Find a way
to do more for others than anyone else
does. Become more valuable. Do more.
Give more. Be more. Serve more.*

—ANTHONY ROBBINS

TRUE WEALTH ISN'T MEASURED BY THE SIZE of your bank account but by the depth of your understanding in using money as a tool for creating meaningful experience, empowering others, and nurturing the seeds of future prosperity. Philosophically speaking, money and wealth go beyond mere accumulation and encompasses aspects like personal fulfillment and joy, long-term sustainability for ourselves, and contribution to others. In essence, real prosperity integrates material success with a purposeful, impactful life.

I am inspired by the various people I interviewed and their approach to money. I also love to read other authors ideas about money. I am open and inspired to take what I can from them, and I hope that you are too.

Take for example, Ramit Sethi, a self-made millionaire I read about recently. He advocates what he calls the "money dial" approach. This philosophy encourages spending extravagantly on what you love and brings you joy while cutting back ruthlessly on what you don't. You turn the money dial down for some things and up for others. "If you love buying books for example," he says, turning the money dial up in that area may mean buying more books or getting a front row seat to see your favorite author speak."

Sethi's approach highlights that money is not just for essentials; it can create meaning and enrich our lives. He suggests that we often limit ourselves by seeing money as merely restrictive, but it's perfectly fine to indulge in things that bring us happiness if we can afford them.

In contrast, other popular authors promote budgeting every penny and encourage that you don't go into debt—to sacrifice today so you can get where you want to be tomorrow. That's also fine for some.

Rachel Rodgers is the author of *We Should All Be Millionaires*. She says, "Here's what you will not see in this book; me telling you to stop drinking your three-dollar latte or to stop being a shopaholic. Here's what I will tell you: how to start making a lot more money."

She believes if you want something—go get it. Work for it. Create another revenue stream. I found her book to be very empowering.

Specific to investing, Anthony Robbins' *Money Master the Game* was deeply impactful to me.

Although I love to hear different opinions from various authors, I don't necessarily agree with everything they say. However, I think authors have a lot to offer us. I love getting those little golden nuggets from reading books, and then I form in my own mind what is right for me. I say,

"Take what you can use and leave the rest."

May you save and use the little golden nuggets from this book.

Money is a powerful tool. It's only when money is more important to us than God that it becomes a snare. Don't let it become a snare. If at any time, our possessions and greed become more important than anything else, that's a problem. My hope for you is that you never allow money to be your God. That's all. It's as simple as that.

The Magic of Compounding: Your Wealth Multiplier

Albert Einstein is credited with saying, "Compound interest is the eighth wonder of the world."

So, for fun, let me ask you . . .

Would you prefer to have $1 million today or one penny that will double every day for 30 days?

GROWTH OF A PENNY THAT DOUBLES DAILY FOR 30 DAYS

DAILY	AMOUNT
Day 1	$ 0.01
Day 2	$ 0.02
Day 3	$ 0.04
Day 4	$ 0.08
Day 5	$ 0.16
Day 6	$ 0.32
Day 7	$ 0.64
Day 8	$ 1.28
Day 9	$ 2.56
Day 10	$ 5.12
Day 11	$ 10.24
Day 12	$ 20.48
Day 13	$ 40.96
Day 14	$ 81.92
Day 15	$ 163.84
Day 16	$ 327.68
Day 17	$ 655.36
Day 18	$ 1,310.72
Day 19	$ 2,621.44
Day 20	$ 5,242.88
Day 21	$ 10,485.76
Day 22	$ 20,971.52
Day 23	$ 41,943.04
Day 24	$ 83,886.08
Day 25	$ 167,772.16
Day 26	$ 335,544.32
Day 27	$ 671,088.64
Day 28	$ 1,342,177.28
Day 29	$ 2,684,354.56
Day 30	$ 5,368,709.12

The main thing this chart illustrates is that compound growth takes time to make a dramatic difference. For the person who wants to have enough money to retire in comfort, starting early is the key to success, even if the starting amount is small.

I share this with you to show the power of compounding your money.

Here is a little fairy tale about the significance compounding can make in your life:

Once upon a time in the bustling city of Financia, there lived a young, ambitious woman named Lily. Lily had a dream of financial independence and prosperity. One day, while scrolling through her favorite financial blogs, she stumbled upon the magic of compounding—the art of making money work for you over time.

Excited by the possibilities, Lily decided to embark on a journey to unlock the power of compounding. She started by diligently saving a portion of her income each month. With her savings in hand, she carefully researched and invested in a diversified portfolio of stocks and bonds. Although the returns were modest at first, Lily remained patient and committed to her financial goals.

As the years passed, something remarkable happened. The compounding magic began to work its wonders. The money Lily had invested started earning returns, not just on the initial amount but also on the returns themselves. It was a snowball rolling down a hill, gathering more and more snow as it went.

Lily continued to contribute to her investments, consistently reinvesting the dividends and interest she earned. The annual returns began to compound at an accelerating rate.

What started as a small stream of income turned into a steady river of wealth.

One day, Lily received a surprise windfall—an unexpected bonus from her job. Instead of splurging on luxuries, she decided to add this surprise bounty to her investment portfolio. This boost turbocharged the compounding process even further.

As the years went by, Lily's wealth grew exponentially. The once modest portfolio had transformed into a substantial nest egg. Lily found herself with the financial freedom to pursue her passions, travel the world, and even start her own business.

Word of Lily's financial success spread, and she became a source of inspiration for others in Financia. The art of compounding, once a mysterious concept, became a guiding principle for many seeking financial independence. The legend of Lily and compounding lived on as a testament to the extraordinary results that could be achieved through the simple act of letting money work its magic over time.

Lily's story teaches us the importance of patience, discipline, and the power of compounding on the journey toward financial success. It's not about getting rich overnight but about making consistent, smart choices throughout the years.

Reader FYI. Multiple articles have been written on this concept, and the question has been asked in various ways.

Crunching the Numbers: Calculating Your Retirement Needs

SEVERAL YEARS AGO, I read Anthony Robbins book, *Money Master the Game*. I highly recommend it. The below is my version of one of his concepts from the book.

What is *your* number for retirement? Make it winnable!

First, write down the number you *think* you need for retirement:

$___________________________

What does security look like for you? How amazing would it feel if these next five things were paid for as long as you live without ever having to work to pay for them again?

1. Your mortgage — for as long as you live, you never have to pay it again.
2. Your utilities —for your home, paid forever.
3. Your food for you and your family —paid forever.
4. Your basic transportation needs – paid forever.
5. Your basic insurance costs—all paid for the rest of your life.

You'd probably feel secure if you could actually do this, right?

Dream 1: Financial Security

I'll bet when we figure these numbers out, your dream of financial security is closer than you think. At least you'll have a reality check, and you will have a close number for what it will take to realize your dreams.

		Per Month
♦	Rent or mortgage payment:	$____________
♦	Gas, electric, water, phone	$____________
♦	Food, household:	$____________
♦	Transportation:	$____________
♦	Insurance:	$____________
♦	**Dream 1 Total:**	$____________

Total basic monthly expenses ________________________x 12 =____________________per year

Take that total number times how many years you think you will live after retirement.

(US average basic annual expenses for a single person: $44,312 as of 2022.)[12] It is usually about 65% of your income. So, on average, you'd need $44,312 x 20 yrs. = $886,240.00 in retirement if you're looking to retire at 60 and live until age 80.

How does this make you feel?

Peace of mind account: Now let's look at what you should have in a side liquid account.

Emergency/Protection Fund: Usually 3-6 months of expenses. But for some, it could be 12 months or more of expenses:

$ ___________________________

Now that you have security and peace of mind achieved, let's talk about:

Dream 2: Financial Exuberance

- Half of your current monthly
  clothing cost $__________
- Half of your current monthly
  dining and entertainment cost $__________
- Half of your small indulgence
  or luxury cost (gym, manicure) $__________
- **Dream 2 Total:** $__________

Total Exuberance monthly expenses ___________________________x
12 = _______________per year

Now add Dream 1 and Dream 2 totals = _______per year you need for exuberance.

Note: You can do half or your whole amount above obviously, depending how much *dream* you want to plan for.

Do the math, and usually the number you need is far less than the number you thought you needed.

Quick Story:

Brionna had always been diligent with her savings, but retirement seemed like a far-off dream. One evening, she sat down with a notebook, determined to figure out how much she would need to retire comfortably. She started by calculating her basic needs: housing, food, healthcare, and other essentials. After crunching the numbers, Brionna determined she would need $40,000 per year to cover her basic expenses. Multiplying this by twenty-five years, she arrived at a nest egg of $1,000,000.

Brionna felt a sense of accomplishment, but something was missing. She thought about her dreams for retirement—traveling the world, taking up new hobbies, and spending quality time with family. She realized that just meeting her basic needs wasn't enough; she wanted to live her *dream* retirement.

Inspired, Brionna began to add her "dream" expenses to the calculation: annual vacations, gourmet cooking classes, a new hobby of painting, and a fund for spontaneous adventures with her grandchildren. She estimated these dreams would require an additional $20,000 per year.

Revisiting her calculations, she now needed $60,000 annually. For 25 years, this totaled $1,500,000. While this number seemed daunting at first, Brionna felt invigorated. She had a clear vision and a specific goal.

With a newfound sense of purpose, Brionna felt ready to take control of her financial future. Her dream retirement was no longer a distant fantasy—it was a concrete goal, and she was determined to achieve it. So, what did she do? She met with a financial planner to create a roadmap.

This story shows the transformation from simply planning for basic needs to envisioning and planning for a dream retirement, resulting in a feeling of empowerment and readiness to achieve the goal.

My point is this:

You are the creator of your life! Create a life you dream of!
Is it time for you to put a plan in place?

Action Steps To Take for Comprehensive Financial Planning

IF SOMEONE APPROACHES ME TODAY seeking a well-rounded financial portfolio, here are the key elements I would recommend considering and implementing:

The Most Obvious: Contribute to your own 401k or Retirement fund. Doing this ONE thing can exponentially catapult you to your retirement goals.

Benefit: You get *free money* from your employer, and you create a habit of contributing to an investment account for your future.

1. **Establish a Financial Plan:**
   + **Action:** Work with a financial planner and create a well-rounded financial plan so that you know if there are any shortfalls to achieving your dreams. Small changes can make a significant difference.
   + **Benefit:** Provides a **clear future to look forward to** and work towards.

2. **Create a Cash Reserve:**
   + **Action:** Establish/maintain a liquid cash account with at least three to six months of expenses, ideally even a year or more. (whatever your comfort level is)
   + **Benefit:** You will **be prepared for life's uncertainties and any great opportunities that come your way.**

3. **Implement Life Insurance:**
   + **Action:** It's the basis of a strong financial portfolio.
   + **Benefit:** It can **provide tax-free cash** to those you leave behind without depleting your investments and other assets. And permanent insurance offers even more.

4. **Invest in the Stock Market:**
   + **Action:** Consult with a financial advisor to determine suitable investments based on how comfortable you are with exposure to the market.
   + **Benefit: Potential for growth** that generally keeps pace with inflation.

5. **Explore Annuities:**
   - **Action:** Consider annuities for your current or future financial strategy.
   - **Benefit:** Provides a **reliable income stream** later in life, as long as it's backed by a strong insurance company.

6. **Invest in Real Estate:**
   - **Action:** Include real estate as part of your diversified financial portfolio.
   - **Benefit:** Offers **diversification of assets** and additional financial options for the future.

7. **Establish Tax-Free Accounts:**
   - **Action:** Set up a Roth account and permanent life insurance to create tax-free income sources.
   - **Benefit: Ensures access to tax-free cash or income. It's one of the very best options to provide yourself certainty!**

8. **Succession and Estate Planning:**
   - **Action: Hire an estate planning attorney to work with your financial planner.** Plan for the transfer of your assets to future generations, focusing on minimizing tax implications.
   - **Benefit:** Grants **freedom to live your desired lifestyle and reduces tax burdens for your heirs.**

9. **Retirement Plans for Business Owners:**
   - **Action:** Implement a SEP, SIMPLE, or 401(k) plan.
   - **Benefit:** Provides **significant tax advantages** and long-term financial security.
   - **Action: Implement permanent life insurance.** It is hands down one of the most powerful things you can do!
   - **Benefit:** Permanent insurance gives you access to cash or guaranteed tax-free income later.

10. **Business Succession Planning:** (We didn't touch on business in the book, so here's a bonus).
   - **Action:** Prepare your business for sale or transfer three to five years in advance, ensuring attractive revenue and expense ratios.
   - **Benefit:** Facilitates a **smooth transition and minimizes tax repercussions** for the next generation.
   - **Action:** When buying or selling property or a business, think about a **Structured Installment Sale Annuity.**
   - **Benefit:** Minimizes capital gains tax as well as income tax. Many don't know about this. It's a powerful tax strategy.

11. **Tax Minimization:**
    - **Action:** Work with a skilled financial planner and accountant to **implement tax-saving strategies throughout your financial journey.**
    - **Benefit: Reduces tax liabilities,** enhancing overall financial health.
    - **By addressing these key areas, you can build a prosperous, resilient financial future.**

NOTES

1   Willis Towers Watson, "Financial Planning for Women," pleasantwealth.com, https://pleasantwealth.com/financial-planning-for-women/.

2   "Earning Women Not Confident with Money." Businessinsider.com, 2023, https://www.businessinsider.com/personal-finance/high-earning-women-not-confident-with-money-2023-7.

3   "Retirement," Transamerica Center for Retirement, transamericaninstitute.org, https://www.transamericaninstitute.org/research/retirement.

4   Katy Chettleburgh, "The Great Wealth Transfer: 3 Things to Consider," bankerslife.com, https://www.bankerslide.com/insights/personal-finance/the-great-wealth-transfer-3-things-to-consider.com/.

5   "Women, Wealth and Investing—A Story of Evolution, morganstanley.com, June 28, 2022, https://www.morganstanley.com/articles/female-invest-women-and-wealth/.

6   "The wealth transfer from baby boomer mostly benefits women," washingtonpost.com, https://www.washingtonpost.com/business/2024/01/16/women-economic-power-demographic-shifts/

7   Pooneh Baghai, Olivia Howard, Lakshmi Prakash, and Jill Zucker, "Women as the next wave of growth in US wealth management," mckinsey.com, July 2020, https://Mckinsey.com/Women as the next wave of growth in US wealth management/.

8   Pooneh Baghi, Olivia Howard, et al.

9   Inyoung Hwang, "A Brief History of the Stock Market," sofi.com, Feb. 27, 2024, https://www.sofi.com/learn/content/history-of-the-stock-market/#:~:text=The%20first%20modern%20stock%20trading%20market%20was%20created%20in%20Amsterdam, Amsterdam%20stock%20exchange%20was%20created.

10   Andrew Beattie, "The Evolution of Stock Exchanges," investopedia.com, Feb. 8, 2024, https://www.investopedia.com/articles/07/stoexchahistory.asp#:~:text=Exchanges%20first%20began%20as%20moneylenders,ranked%20by%20total%20market%20capitalization.

11   Jennifer Lobb and Heidi Gollub, "Life insurance statistics and industry trends 2024, usatoday.com, Jan.24, 2024, https://www.usatoday.com/money/blueprint/life-insurance/life-insurance-statistics/#:~:text=Key%20points,the%20life%20insurance%20they%20need.

NEXT STEPS

READY TO TAKE IT TO THE NEXT LEVEL?

I work with people who are committed to solving what truly matters most and are eager to reach the next level of financial success. I partner with those who share a serious drive to grow their wealth and secure their future. I would love for that to be you.

Let's start the conversation:
https://www.conniecostanzo.com

Connect with me on LinkedIn:
https://www.linkedin.com/in/connie-costanzo/

Stay in touch with me on Facebook:
https://www.facebook.com/connie.costanzo.10

GET YOUR BONUS GIFT!

I'd like to offer you an exclusive bonus where we'll explore strategies beyond this book to help you experience the lifestyle and retirement of your dreams—whether that's savoring a 12-course tasting menu at world-class restaurants, traveling in luxury, supporting family, or giving back to causes you care about.

With these strategies, you'll gain the clarity and confidence to take control of your financial future without the stress of doing it all yourself. Here's a sneak peek at what we'll cover:

- Simple, done-for-you solutions to eliminate financial stress and stay confident, no matter what happens in the market or your life.

- Smart investments that can lower your risk and help you grow wealth, even during market downturns.

- How to stop overpaying taxes on your income, investments and beyond, potentially saving $100,000s or $1,000,000s over time.

- And much more!

Register at: ConnieCostanzo.com/Gift
or scan the QR code to get your
BONUS GIFT!

If this book has helped you, I would love to hear your comments. Please message me on LinkedIn and tag me @Connie Costanzo.

ACKNOWLEDGMENTS

THANK YOU TO PHIL, my amazing husband, who puts me on a pedestal I certainly don't belong on but aspire to. I will forever love you for seeing in me what I don't always see in myself and being my rock when I need it. You are the love of my life!

To the rest of my family who inspire me to be more and do more. Luigi, you are always positive and a good leader, and I'm so proud of you. Amy, you always bring a smile to my face and warmth to my heart. Nino, you are my sunshine, and I admire your gift of always seeing the good in circumstances and in people. You bring that ray of hope to others and to me. Filippo, your heart for others is truly inspiring and brings tears to my eyes sometimes, and Alyssa, how happy I am to have you in our lives now. I look forward to many memorable, fun times with you. And to my amazing, beautiful Brionna, who brings more than *everything* I ever wanted in a daughter. You are so special to me! To Luigi, Leanna, and Elianora, who I love to pieces.

You shine in my heart. My prayer is that you will go into the world and use your gifts to do what you are meant to do. I hope each of you knows the fullness of my love for you and the *joy* you bring to my life! Thank you all for your support!

To my mom and dad, my brothers, Guy, Dan and Greg, and my amazing sisters, Cathy, Sandy, and Kim. I would not be the person I am today without each of you. It has been a pleasure to see how you each deal with money. You have taught me much without even knowing it. I treasure the family we are and the support you always give me. Nothing is greater! I love each of you more than you know. I thank all my in-laws. You are incredibly special, and you bring such great gifts to our family. I love you as well! To my nieces and nephews. You rock! I hope this book inspires you to become good money managers.

To Robyn Crane, a mentor and coach, for "stretching" me out of my comfort zone (in a major way) and for letting me "borrow your belief" for a little while. You inspire me, and I'm so grateful to have you in my life! You will never know the full impact you have had on me.

To Amber Chapman, my first editor, who helped get this book started. You took my words and wove them into something people could understand. And to Gail Kerzner, my editor whose wisdom and encouragement I can never repay. I can't thank you enough for your knowledge, support, thoughtful words, and insight. I hope you know how much I appreciate you. This book would not have been as clear or powerful without your input. You are gracious and kind. I thank you from the bottom of my heart!

To the wonderful men and women who shared their personal stories about money. You shared because you wanted to make an impact. I can't thank you enough.

To my existing clients, who I have the honor and privilege of serving. I truly love working for and with you. Thank you for your faith in me. Let's journey forward, growing stronger and achieving more every step of the way.

Thank you to my readers. I hope hearing these stories inspire you and that you implement one or two strategies so that you can have the life you dream of!

And the biggest thank you to God, my Father! Thank you for believing in me and for loving me. I'm so grateful for the gifts you give me, for always being there for me, and expanding my mind and my vision for what we can do hand-in-hand. I love You!

ABOUT THE AUTHOR

CONNIE COSTANZO is a highly sought-after financial planner, dedicated to empowering high-achieving executive women in building and protecting their wealth. Her passion lies in fostering financial security and long-term independence, enabling her clients to live rich, fulfilling lives.

With over twenty years of experience in the Financial Services Industry, Connie serves as a Financial Planner at Ascend Wealth Management, LLC. Her extensive background, including her tenure as a business owner, gives her a unique perspective in addressing her clients' financial needs. Connie's expertise provides readers with actionable insights for achieving financial security and building lasting wealth.

Connie, a long-time resident of Brunswick, OH, is deeply connected to her community. She is happily married, the proud mother of four grown children, and blessed with two wonderful daughters-in-law and three grandchildren who never cease to inspire her.

In addition to her family, Connie serves on three boards: NAWBO (National Association of Women Business Owners), the Northern Medina County Chamber Alliance, and the Northern Medina County Chamber Charities Board, where she continues to contribute her expertise and passion for community growth. She also serves her parish in Brunswick, Ohio.

On weekends, you'll often find her enjoying time outdoors riding through the parks or traveling to Amish Country on her Honda 500 Rebel, side-by-side with her husband on his Honda 750 Shadow.

Advisory Services offered through Ascend Wealth Management, LLC, a Registered Investment Advisor.